Understanding China

The series will provide you with in-depth information on China's social, cultural and economic aspects. It covers a broad variety of topics, from economics and history to law, philosophy, cultural geography and regional politics, and offers a wealth of materials for researchers, doctoral students, and experienced practitioners.

Maria Francesca Staiano

Chinese Law and Its International Projection

Building a Community with a Shared Future for Mankind

Springer

Maria Francesca Staiano
Center on China Studies of the International Relations Institute
National University of La Plata
La Plata, Buenos Aires, Argentina

ISSN 2196-3134 ISSN 2196-3142 (electronic)
Understanding China
ISBN 978-981-19-9577-4 ISBN 978-981-19-9578-1 (eBook)
https://doi.org/10.1007/978-981-19-9578-1

This Springer imprint is published by the registered company Springer Nature Singapore Pte Ltd.
The registered company address is: 152 Beach Road, #21-01/04 Gateway East, Singapore 189721, Singapore

To my husband Dario and my daughter Demetra.
The value of a man and the inspiration of mother Earth, always with me.

Foreword

I know Dr. Francesca for more than one decade. She is a serious scholar bridging different countries and civilizations. Her study and writing on China are closer to the fact and always enlightening. I really appreciate her expertise on comparative studies and the spirit for promotion of exchanges between countries and peoples.

Analysing Chinese law is not a simple task. China is a millenary civilization, one of the oldest and deciphering this cultural universe hidden within legal norms requires profound attention to all the literary, pictorial and scientific manifestations of China.

The content of international law in peace and rule of law thinking is not only related to deepening reform, opening up, and promoting China's economic development and social progress, but also to the overall international landscape. Global governance and peace are related to the various opportunities and challenges that promote development. As China approaches the centre of the world stage, it represents the largest developing country, and its position, attitude, proposal, and contribution to international law are conspicuous and have become more extensive and impactful. China's comprehensive governance of the country in accordance with the law has entered a track of clearer goals, more comprehensive content, and more scientific paths, with better and faster development.

The most important change is Xi Jinping's thoughts on the rule of law and his proposals on international law. Its basis and background is China's reform and opening up, Marxist legal research that is based on practice, combining theory with practice, taking into account the country's national conditions and the reality of international society. Another fundamental axis is the trend of development of human society. Looking back at the past 40 years, the most certain reality in the world development process is the word "change", and the biggest trend is to seek peace.

At the start of the reform and opening up in 1980, China was still in the low-level human development group, entered the middle level human development group after 1995; China's human development index after 2010 began to exceed the world average and reached a high level of human development in 2011. From the low-level human category in 1990, among 47 countries, China is the only country that has changed its destination through development and has successfully entered the high-level human development group. The country's human development has been reflected in the reduction of poverty, improving income, health and education, which is reflected behind the Human Development Index in China. Reform and opening up have made China a rapid and miraculous "big change" in its development, making China the world's second-largest economy and placing China at the forefront of sustainable development, technological innovation and application, and the most dynamic market.

If the restoration of the People's Republic of China's (PRC's) lawful seat in the United Nations in 1971 was regarded as the beginning of China's political integration into the world family, the Beijing Olympic Games in 2008 was a symbol of China's wider and deeper cultural integration into the world, and the successful accession to the World Trade Organization (WTO) in 2001 was another milestone of China's integration into economic globalization. In 2001, China successfully joined the World Trade Organization, which was another milestone in China's integration into economic globalisation in the field of international economics and trade.

On October 29, 2020, the Fifth Plenary Session of the 19th Central Committee of the Communist Party of China approved the Five-Year Plan and Proposals for 2035. This important document that links the past and the future indicates that China is at the decisive stage for building a moderately prosperous society in all aspects. At this time, significant progress has been made in the comprehensive governance of the country in accordance with the law, significant achievements have been made in international governance.

Maria Francesca Staiano's book brings together these two aspects, the internal evolution of the implementation of the rule of law in China, and the influence of international law as a source of Chinese domestic law, adding a totally innovative one. The return of the Chinese experience on a global level, as a promoter of peace and development in international relations, is encouraging.

Liu Huawen
Deputy Director and Researcher
of the Institute of International Law
of the Chinese Academy of Social
Sciences (CASS)
Beijing, China

Premise

The book aims to explore the construction of Chinese law, with an evolution that has been strongly inspired by international law, that has functioned as a "pioneer of legal civilization" in China. Chinese law is a fluid sedimentation of traditional elements of Chinese culture and the internalisation of external elements. Currently in China we are witnessing a strengthening of concepts traditionally belonging to a Western matrix, such as *democracy*, *human rights*, *rule of law*, but in an innovative way, "with Chinese characteristics". In China a two-phase system has been generated: on the one hand, we have a descending phase from international and foreign law that have been adopted as a model in China (Civil Law system), and an ascending phase deriving from the Chinese "declination" of these elements which then fall under international law with new guises, taking on innovative meanings.

The internal dimension of Chinese legal evolution, therefore, coincides with a progressive incursion also at the international level, questioning the traditional rules of international relations: the most relevant and comprehensive concept that has been proposed by China in recent years is certainly the idea of building a "community with a shared future for mankind". This aspiration demonstrates a global and integral vocation of international law capable of embracing relations of a new type, towards a multipolar democratisation of international relations, which mark the need for the beginning of a new era. According to Xi Jinping, "Countries vary in history, culture, system and economic development level, but peoples of all countries uphold the shared human values of peace, development, equity, justice, democracy and freedom".[1]

This common aspiration, the need to generate a symbiotic, empathic and understanding international community of the other is the drive that gave birth to this book. Not "China and the others", not "China as a separate universe", but Chinese characteristics as a cultural form supplementing current international law, which spills over into international relations. The sense of justice that makes us "endure" positive law, therefore, becomes a common element, a new instrument of international dialogue

[1] Keynote speech delivered by Xi Jinping at the Communist Party of China and World Political Parties Summit. July 6, 2021.

in which the interlocutors come from contexts hitherto considered peripheral: Asia, Latin America and Africa. China, therefore, as the driving force behind these new spaces of interpretation of the "old" and creator of innovative reworkings capable of deconstructing and rebuilding a more just and equitable global order.

Contents

Chapter 1
Traditional Elements in the Chinese Legal System

1.1 Legal Tradition: The Evolution from the *Sinic* Legal System to the *Chinese* Legal System

Law is always the product of a reference culture, a distinctive sign of the idea of justice that a particular civilization has matured over the course of its history. Justice is one of the traditional cornerstones on which the very concept of law (*Ius*) is based, in fact it shares the etymological genesis (*Iustum, iustitia*). Justice, as a legal idea, is also linked to good or evil, thus linking it to an ethical interpretation (Zoja, 2007).

To analyse Chinese law, therefore, we need to draw on the strict relationship between law, language, culture and tradition in China. The Chinese legal system uses structures and institutes that Western legal systems do not use, and language is of fundamental importance in effectively understanding that. Many authors speak of a constant "ambiguity" of the Chinese legal language that generates many difficulties for the foreign investigator, but this "ambiguity" is every legal civilization's characteristic.

The Chinese language is based on characters, ideograms and pictograms, symbols that represent the threshold between the imaginary, the symbolic and the real. According to the Chinese painter and poet Shitao (1642–1707)[1] "The uniqueness of the stroke is the origin of all beings, the root of the ten thousand forms". Entering the Chinese legal cultural experience, therefore, means setting out to discover one's own idea of law, ethics and justice in line with a philosophy and a general theory of law that starts from values, images and representations different from those of the West. It is in this sense that the definition of "Chinese characteristics" takes on relevance, an expression that directs us to the study of Chinese sciences through two warnings. On the one hand, it is necessary to take into consideration the Chinese civilization in its specific evolution, albeit also influenced by foreign elements; on the other hand, to get out of a Westernised dominant narrative, encountering "another thought different not so much for its contents, but for the way it is elaborated [...]

[1] Shitao is the name by which the poet Zhu Ruoji is known.

M. F. Staiano, *Chinese Law and Its International Projection*, Understanding China,
https://doi.org/10.1007/978-981-19-9578-1_1

avoiding the only apparently tolerant superficiality that consists in reducing every tradition to our standard "culturalism", inspired by a hermeneutic *koiné* of presumed universal concepts and thoughts which in reality are nothing more than ideological games"(Sini, 2012: 56).

According to Professor Mi Jian, it is necessary to differentiate between "Sinic legal system" and "modern legal system" (Mi, 2005). The Sinic juridical system proposes itself as "the Sinic juridical tradition (*Zhonghua faxi*) which on the basis of traditional Chinese thought created the national juridical system and influenced the juridical systems of the nations that suffered the infuelty of China" (Mi, 2005: 13).

According to Professors Mi (2005) and Yang (2005), the Sinic juridical system had several characteristics: (a) the unity of rites and punishments; (b) law as a derivation from the sovereign; (c) inequality in law; (d) union of administration and jurisdiction.

The Chinese legal system was inspired by traditional cultural values that originate in Confucian ethics. Anne Cheng deals with Confucian thought with extreme depth, analysing the concept of 義 (*yi*), the "sense of what is right": "the whole content of the notion of *yi* as a *sense of right* includes *justice* but also *rightness*, that is the perception of what is appropriate to a particular circumstance, of what is appropriate to do in a given situation", and in an individualised key, containing the ideogram of *yi* also the ideogram of *me* (我, *wo*). This is associated with the concept of rite (禮, *li*), which represents the "significant act par excellence" (Cheng, 2000: 61). Therefore, the *ritual spirit* and the *sense of what is right* are the founding elements of Confucian ethics, to be implemented in a personal and pragmatic way, and not in the Western transcendental sense (Cheng, 2000: 62). The implementation rituals of *yi* still today constitute the idea according to which *li* are opposed to the traditional conception of law 法 (*fa*), understood as positivist concept of law, made of coercitive implementation through sanctions.

This arrangement has clearly divided civil law, organised according to *li*, and criminal law, ensured according to the punishments of the *fa*. Rites and punishments therefore guaranteed the law. "The rites forbid the performance of an action, the laws punish the action performed" (Mi, 2005: 15).

These values are inspired by a precise hierarchy between moral principles towards a harmonious balance. But the great distinction of the traditional value system of the PRC is that it is based on the inequality of forces, the primacy of collective rights over individual rights, of social harmony over individual freedom, of the duty to work with respect to the right to work, state control of the economy with respect to the free market, respect for political leadership with respect to political disaffection, family relations with respect to the disintegration of the family. Today we call these values "Asian Values", based on the Asian Regional Declaration held in Bangkok in 1993 (Sen, 2001).

1.2 Origins of the Conception of the Rule of Law in China

According to Professor Yang (2005), "Law is the bearer of a series of values linked to the cultural tradition of a people, which is at the basis of the formation of its juridical tradition. However, once established, it too conditions the global development of a people's culture. A central role in this process is played by philosophical thought, which penetrates culture and law and therefore determines its legal tradition".

An expression interpreted as "Rule of law" in Chinese culture begins with Confucius (551–479 BC) who speaks of 法治 (*fazhi*), rule by law, as opposed to 人治 (*renzhi*), rule by man. For Confucius, and later his disciple Mencius (372–279 BC), it is the feeling of humanity (Rén) that governs the actions and relationships of men, and for this reason they opposed the new currents of thought that at that time (the period of the warring states) tried to overcome traditional values through a bureaucratization of power, with written laws. Many scholars have interpreted the Confucian doctrine of "government by men" as the original cause of the dictatorship of the Emperors, which in fact was criticised and tried to destroy during the Cultural Revolution of the years 1966–1976 (Costa & Zolo, 2002: 739). This interpretation of the concept of 人治 (*renzhi*) is not correct if we think of the strictly philosophical activity that Confucius and his disciples developed, towards a political, social and moral theorization of the State. The concept of 人治 (*renzhi*) is comfortable with Plato's "policy of the good man", that is, a virtuous man, whose virtue was represented by the "just average", a balance, a fair measure of the just and the good in policy life (Kramer, 1996). What Confucius and Mencius sponsored was the government by a good, valuable man, who had a feeling of benevolence towards his citizens and not of force, to express himself through penalties and sanctions established by law. What the school of Confucianism proposes, and which was implemented for a long time because it was chosen by several Emperors in the history of China, is a "government of virtue" of "rituals", which was inspired by the "common good" of the people, to their interests. The "love towards the people" then signs an intellectual political movement, which is still studied as Chinese "humanism" (Costa & Zolo, 2002: 747).

The rites or rituals have their roots even earlier than in Confucianism: they were born in the primitive ceremonies of the tribal clans before the Xia dynasty, in 2100 BC. After only ceremonial use, the Li spread in the Xia and Shang dynasties, implementing themselves as an all-encompassing political and social system, reaching its maximum strength under the Xi Zhou dynasty (1100–771 BC). In the Xi Zhou dynasty, rituals represented everything: they regulated cultural ceremonies, ordinances, penalties, customs, ethics, family relations and social hierarchy. From the Han dynasty (206 BC–220 AD) the rituals entered the written law and were adopted in jurisdictional decisions. Under the Tang dynasty (618–907), an entire Legal Code was drawn up in line with the rites, and this legal tradition remained unchanged until the late Qing dynasty (1644–1911). However, it should be noted that during the Han dynasty Confucianism and Legalism coexisted under the principle "government by men through law" (Costa & Zolo, 2002: 754). This means that the rites dominated the legal and political scene in China from the first century to the end of the nineteenth century, for 1900 years: this phenomenon is still visible in social relations in China.[2]

The importance of the rites is evident if we think that they survived historical stages radically different from the Chinese Humanism of Confucius. For example, Confucius thought that the rites represented a fundamental tool for the political system, and what he proposed was basically the virtue of the rulers, the importance of education, after an economic improvement of the conditions of the citizens (Costa & Zolo, 2002: 750–755). These axes were followed by Mao Zedong and Deng Xiaoping, although according to different modalities, towards a modernization of internal and international politics to reach a way out of the extreme poverty and agricultural and cultural backwardness that China was experiencing, sometimes through strict and harsh policies, such as the "great leap forward" or the one-child policy.[3]

Likewise, in opposition to the law, Confucius said that sanctions and penalties do not touch the spirit of the people, but that by guiding the people with the laws, the penalties standardize the people, without a sense of personal involvement; instead, guiding the people with virtues, the rituals uniform the people, generating a sense of collective shame. The feeling of "shame" is still visible in China not only at the level of interpersonal and international relations, with the typical expressions "lose face" or "put on face", but also at the level of example of the virtues of the rulers, if we think about the anti-corruption campaign that is being carried out in the PRC, and that represents one of the main axes of Xi Jinping's policy, closely related to the implementation of the rule of law.

1.3 Humanism or Not Humanism?

As masterfully described by Moore, "The Chinese tradition of thought and culture can be characterised by humanism, by its emphasis on the ethical, the intellectual (mainly in relation to life and activity), the aesthetic and the social" (Moore, 1968: 8).

According to Confucius, "man has a sacred mission: to reaffirm and elevate his humanity more and more" (Cheng, 2000: 62). Man as the centre of philosophical speculation in ancient China generated the definition of Confucian doctrine in terms of "humanism" (Grecchi, 2009). The indissoluble link between philosophy and human relations, and the pragmatic social action of Confucianism, have led to a direct interest of Chinese thinkers and scholarly officials, towards politics and governance in terms of harmonious social stability. The "feeling of humanity" (*ren*, 仁)

[2] For an in-depth explanation on the subject, which is not possible now due to the purpose of this work, Costa P. – Zolo D., *Lo stato di diritto: storia, teoria, critica*, 2002, Feltrinelli.

[3] To deepen the subject: Staiano M.F., *La Ley sobre la población y la planificación familiar de la RPC: un camino de desarrollo del sistema jurídico interno chino en el marco del derecho internacional*, en *El ordenamiento jurídico de la República Popular China en el marco del Derecho Internacional: planificación familiar, migraciones y cooperación*, 2014, Instituto de Relaciones Internacionales- UNLP Press.

manifested through the rites, therefore, responds to the need to "perfect oneself in order to rule men", 修己 治 人 (*xiuji zhiren*) as detailed by Zhu Xi (Cheng, 2000: 548). The strong political and social influence of Confucian thought can easily be identified in terms of the "formation of man", not only in a pedagogical key but above all in a legal one (Staiano, 2016; Moore, 1968: 6). It is with Mencius[4] that an even more humanistic impulse will be given to Confucian thought, not only through a deeper conviction about the benevolent nature of the human being, but also by extending the latter, perceiving "the continuity between Heaven and Man within of a morality derived directly from nature" (Cheng, 2000: 290) and arguing "the need for Confucian humanism to be transferred to a broader context to assume its meaning more comprehensively" (Cheng, 2000: 290).

In fact, an essential element of Chinese humanism is given by the encounter between Confucianism and Taoism, which allowed the penetration of human nature in the environmental context in which it is inserted, that is, "that context of Chinese humanism that consists in the symbiosis of man with the universe, it allowed the fusion between these two philosophical currents "(Grecchi, 2009: 35; Cheng, 2000). As also held by Chan Wing-tsit "The opposition between humanistic Confucianism and naturalistic Taoism is, at first glance, almost irreconcilable. But any complete distinction inevitably distorts the picture. Early Taoism is closer to Confucianism than is generally understood, especially in its philosophy of life" (Chan, 1968b: 31). It is no coincidence that the redefined concept of *Tianxia* (天下) constitutes the apex of this union, representing "everything under the sky" and including all beings and non-beings, each with its own political, cosmological and energetic, institutional and moral function.[5] Then the neo-Confucians (eleventh-twelfth centuries) synthesised the concept of "heavenly principle" (天理) which, by regulating the universe through its moral nature, "equates to the highest Confucian virtue, *ren* (仁), 'love of neighbour', which should no longer be understood as referring only to humanity, but extends to the entire universe. The universal value of *ren* (仁) and the existence of a single entity (一体) that would cancel out any difference between the nature of the cosmos and the nature of man merge into a single Principle, which can take different forms (理 一 而 分 殊)" (Scarpari, 2019). Chan Wing-tsit states that "the closest statement to a definition of *ren* (仁) is that it consists in mastering oneself and returning to ownership: this is practically equivalent to all Confucian philosophy, since *ren*, thus defined, implies the realisation of the self and the creation of a social order" (Chan, 1968b: 33).

---

[4] Pre-Qin philosopher who developed his activities in the times of Guanzi, Laozi, Confucius, Mozi, Xunzi and Hanfeizi. It belonged to the school of Legalism, which –among other postulates- proposed a direct connection between morality and interstate order (Yan, Xuetong, *Ancient Chinese Thought, Modern Chinese Power*, Princeton University Press, 2011).

[5] For a deepening of the notion of *Tianxia,* Staiano M.F.-Bogado Bordazar L., *Las teorías de las relaciones internacionales con "características chinas" y sus implicaciones en América Latina,* in Staiano & Bordazar (Coordinators), *Dossier especial sobre China: China y su proyección en el siglo XXI, Revista de Relaciones Internacionales,* Vol. 26, N. 53, Universidad Nacional de La Plata Press, December 2017.

Interestingly, many western authors argue that we cannot speak of Chinese humanism, given the extreme cultural difference and historical remoteness of the periods in the west and in China and in the name of a "too immediate and lazy humanistic universalism" (Jullien, 2011: 31), while others speak of a dehumanisation of Confucianism due to the westernisation of China (Grecchi, 2009: 40). However, there is no doubt that "in China, the note of humanism has been strong, not only in Confucianism, but also in Taoism and Buddhism. It is not necessary to continue arguing that humanism is the keynote of Chinese thought. That keynote vibrates throughout the history of China" (Chan, 1968b: 22).

Now, the Chinese humanistic spirit, through the values of Confucian and Taoist thoughts, lasts from the sixth century B.C. until today. However, the hybridization of China due to the initial collision with the colonial West, today has favoured a social openness to certain instances of the population, adapting to the new needs arising from the development of the last forty years and the progressive internationalisation of the country. Therefore, domestically and internationally, we are witnessing an affirmation of innovative principles and a crisis between Western human rights and Asian values, subsumed in "Chinese characteristics". Already in the 1960s, in fact, the development of a peculiar "scientific humanism" had been observed in China (Irti, 2017), as a representative of this *unicum*, due to the western impact that has generated crucial changes at the epistemological and philosophical level (Chan, 1968b: 67).

1.4 Roman Law in Chinese Law: "Double Philosophical Tradition" System

While Roman law was forged by the philosophy of natural law (*ziranfa*), ancient Chinese law is based on the philosophical tradition of "unity between heaven and man" (*tian ren he yi*) (Yang, 2005: 30). Natural law penetrated into Roman law, characterised by the foray of the philosophy of the Athenian Stoics into Rome in the second century BC., through the work of Panezio who took root in the Scipionic Circle. Stoicism had within itself the humanistic characteristics made explicit by the values of *public utility, solidarity* and *equality* (Yang, 2005: 33). This inheritance accepted by Cicero was transmitted in the philosophical structure of Roman law, sanctioning the denial of the supremacy of the state over the individual, "because the *res publica* arises from a contract concluded between people who want to ensure mutual protection" (Yang, 2005: 33).

As affirmed by Schipani:

> Roman law draws its principle from the foundation of Rome and concludes the era of its formation with the codes of Justinian and his jurists (*Codex, Digesta, Institutiones*), produced by the convergence of the ruling of the legislator and the elaboration of the *iuris scientia*. In these codes, the unity and internal consonant of law was brought to perfection, to create a *ius Romanum comune*, developed as a 'system' that includes everything, from its *principium*. These codes were destined to be disseminated *ad omnes populos* and in *omne aevum* (to

> all peoples, in all epochs), and they transferred to us those concepts, principles, institutes, rules, and that method of preliminary and abstract elaboration cases, and the consequences connected to them on the basis of verifiable rationes in relation to men (Dig., 1, 5, 2), the result of constant discussion and commitment to daily improvement, by jurists (Dig., 1, 2, 2, 13).
>
> (Schipani, 2009)

Through the "domination of rationality" (*lixing de tongzhi*), Roman law gave a foundation to the superiority of natural law over the legal norm, which is therefore binding and effective only and in terms of a relationship of non-contradiction with it. This "right reason" (*zhengque de lixing*) constitutes an imperishable and constant right, with *erga omnes* application, which will lay the foundations for the philosophical theory of human rights in the West (Yang: 35). As summarised by Yang, the Roman tradition was based on at least six characteristics: (a) the sacrosanct faith in justice, as the supreme principle to be pursued in order to achieve good; (b) the faithful cult of reason, in terms of "natural reason"; (c) the critique of effective law, through a dialectic between the ideal to be pursued and the applicative reality of law; (d) the pursuit of equality; (e) the clear conception of the contract, from which they are derived not only in the concept of "consensual contract", but also the future "social contract" in politics; (f) the government of law that is respectful of human personality, that is, based on fundamental rights and their protection (Yang, 2005).

We can note, therefore, that a parallelism between the philosophical tradition of Roman law and ancient Chinese law is possible only in terms of "clear opposition" between the two systems. In fact, since the Tang dynasty (618–907 AD) the main characteristics of ancient Chinese law were: "unity of rites and punishments; derivation of the law only from the sovereign; inequality of people by law; union of administration and jurisdiction; absence of a dialectic between ideal law and effective law; attempt at conciliation to avoid judgement; administration through morals according to the three principles *generosity and understanding for the other, teaching and persuading, goodness and rigour*" (Schipani, 2005: 58).

However, as stated by Jiang (2005ab: 49) in the Europe of the fourteenth-sixteenth centuries the era of the "Three Rs" was established: *Renaissance, Religious Reform and Rediscovery of Roman law*. These three variables have in common the humanistic element, understood as the development of a people-centred conception, and above all they will have relevance in the evolution of the concept of "socialist market economy" in China (Jiang, 2005b).

The civil law system as the basis of modern Chinese law has meant the recognition by China of the importance of the Roman legal tradition. Roman law, therefore, constitutes an essential pillar in the construction of the Chinese legal system. According to Professor Jiang Ping "legal culture can be inherited, and therefore the legal heritage of Roman law can also be inherited and used in modern China" (Jiang, 2005a: 4). The choice of Roman law was fundamentally inspired by two factors: (a) the social meaning of Roman law, transferable to the socialist legal experience; (b) the rationality of the Roman private law system (Jiang, 2005b). For this reason, we can define Chinese law as a dual-tradition system: on the one hand, traditional Chinese elements from antiquity to contemporaneity; on the other, the legacy of Roman law with its essential characters of codification and constitutionalisation. Both traditions have settled into Chinese legal culture, to the point of generating the need for a "rule of law with Chinese characteristics".

There were two turning points for the modernization of Chinese law: (a) the Opium Wars (1840–1842); (b) the constitution of the People's Republic of China.

The Opium Wars marked the transition from the ancient age of Chinese law as a "closed" sinic system to modern Chinese law, open, albeit "by force", generating a "process of assimilation and fusion between the two Chinese legal cultures and Western" (Ding, 2005: 101) up to the choice of Civil law as the legal model to follow. In fact, both the experience of neighbouring Japan, which had already incorporated German law, and the officials sent during the last Qing dynasty, had learned that the Roman system would bring considerable advantages, especially in terms of systematisation of law.

The proclamation of the People's Republic marked the beginning of a typically Chinese process but no longer closed and isolated, as it was inspired by international integration. However, this process cannot "free itself" from that Romanistic legacy that was consolidated until 1949. In fact, "China began studying the continental legal system, and trying to apply it, since the end of the Qing period (1644–1911) "and" in the period of the Republic (1911–1949) the continental legal system, in its foundations and in its concrete systems, had already substantially established itself" (Ding, 2005: 102; Schipani, 2005: 59). In a first phase, following the proclamation of the People's Republic, Mao Zedong sanctioned "the irreconcilability and opposition between socialism and capitalism" (Ding, 2005: 102), abolishing all the laws established in the nationalist period and starting the institutional political process and law of New China. However, the millennial legal tradition of the Sinic system and the subsequent "Romanization" of Chinese law due to the clash-encounter with the West represented a profound legal culture of which New China has preserved many legacies.

But if this is the "modern" legacy of Roman law in the Chinese legal system, from hundreds of previous years it is the impact that Roman law, and other foreign legal traditions, had on Chinese cultural heritage through the two Silk Roads. In fact, as many scholars have now pointed out, the Silk Road was not only the one that linked the city of Xi'an with European continent, in particular up to Rome, but also that of the trans pacific trade route of the 'Manila Galleon' which from 1565 to 1815 he connected East and West through Hispanic America. In this sense, we can identify a soft-approach of foreign cultures with China, preceding the "collision" that then occurred with the West of modern states.

1.5 The Two Silk Routes: An Ancient Way to Globalisation of Law?

The Silk Road that linked China to Europe, passing through Eurasia, has generated a profound dialogue between ancient civilizations, through an intense osmotic exchange between different cultures not only from an economic-commercial point of view, but above all cultural and legal (Fig. 1.1). As described by Millward (2013), quoted by Villagrán (2019), "The expression 'Silk Road' refers to more than the silk trade between China and Rome over a few centuries. It represents the exchange of objects and ideas, both intentional and Western, that took place through trade, diplomacy, conquests, migrations, and pilgrimages that intensified the integration of the Afro-Eurasian continent from the Neolithic to the Middle Ages. Warriors, missionaries, nomads, emissaries, and artisans, as well as merchants, contributed to the continuous inter-fertilization in this space, which flourished in periods of imperial and religious unification."

The Silk Road was actually a collection of multiple land and sea routes, used not only to exchange goods, but also ideas, technologies and knowledge between populations of different cultures: a multidimensional line of communication active since the first century BC. Then it was the Han dynasty that opened the empire to other countries to encourage trade and contacts with Rome began, which deepened with Augustus. "Rome and the Chinese Empire never came into direct contact because they were separated by two great empires, the Parthian Empire and the Kushana

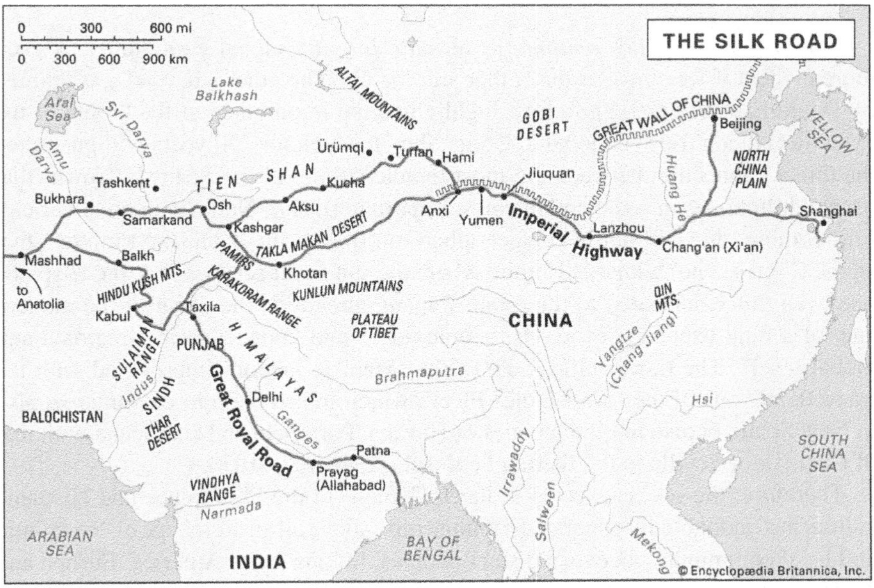

Fig. 1.1 *Source* Encyclopedia Britannica

Empire, even though there were some attempts on both sides to make direct contact by sending ambassadors. Some speak of this network of roads, "caravan routes" as a form of archaic globalisation" (Caselli, 2019). It is interesting to note how Rome was called by the Chinese: Da Qin, the great China. On the contrary for the Romans the Chinese were the Seres, a word that derives from *serica*, with which silk is called. Although the two empires had not known each other directly, both had a mythicized representation of each other, as large political and commercial empires wrapped in a sort of "mystery" (Caselli, 2019). Suffice it to say that the city of Liqian was founded for Roman legionaries and only in 592 AD, It was "incorporated into the Fanmu district by Emperor Wendi (581–604)" (Cardilli, 2019). "Up until 592 AD, therefore, Liqian, for about six centuries, had enjoyed autonomy and independence in the structure of the Chinese empire, being able to regulate the relations of its citizens with its own customs, while having to participate in the common defence against the incursions of nomadic peoples of Central Asia and contributing to the security of the 'Silk Road'" (Cardilli, 2019). From this small example we can easily deduce the inclusive capacity generated by the experiment of political, juridical and multi-ethnic coexistence with a security function of the Silk Road, of the city of Lijiang. Indeed, as brilliantly explained by Cardilli:

> It is, therefore, a juridical-political solution that respects the specificity of the community of foreign men captured and deported to the Chinese Empire, recognizing them the 'privilege' of founding a new city in a territory of the Chinese Empire in order to serve the security objectives of the Empire. These are fundamental questions for understanding the inclusive mechanisms intended to strengthen the stability of great political realities in history, such as the Roman Empire on one side and the Chinese Empire on the other.
> (Cardilli, 2019: 59).

This approach of *ius gentium*, as an *ante litteram* global community, is even more evident if we consider the "other silk road". "The other silk road", as defined by David Esborraz (2018), in fact, highlighted the importance of the "route of the 'Manila Galleon' (also called the 'China Ship'), which for 250 years will guarantee the direct connection between the most remote colony of the Spanish Crown (that of the Philippines, in Asia) and the most important (that of New Spain, in America). Furthermore, this will put in contact, albeit informally, the 'Celestial Empire' (that is, the Chinese one) with the 'Empire where the sun never sets' (that is, the Hispanic one). All this contributed to the establishment, already at the dawn of the modern age, of a fluid exchange of goods, people, ideas and knowledge at a regional and global level". The transpacific route of the 'Manila Galleon' intertwined with the transatlantic one of the 'West Indies Fleet', which linked the port of Veracruz, also in New Spain, or also the Indian ones of Havana, Portobelo and Cartagena with that of Cadiz or of Seville in the Iberian Peninsula (Esborraz, 2018).

Therefore, the coexistence of Indians, Chinese in the Philippines and Hispanic culture has undoubtedly generated a unique mix, above all an archetype of "economic and legal community" between distant peoples, linking Asia, America, Europe and Africa.

As described by Zhao Tingyang with the metaphor of the "Chinese vortex": "China has expanded thanks to the invaders. Quite the opposite of the West" (Zhao, 2022).

Indeed, the concept of *Tianxia*, recently reworked by Zhao Tingyang, perfectly describes the link between the one and the whole, between the national and the international, between the theoretical and the practical. As a concrete *pax perpetua* solution, the Silk Roads were the concrete, experienced materialisation of the multiplicity contained in the *Tianxia*. Furthermore, this concept has the virtue of bringing the three great spiritual drives closer together: Buddhism, Taoism and Confucianism. Indeed, there are numerous aspects of convergence between these three schools of thought and the Chinese approach to social coexistence, an archetype necessary for the development of law, is the integration between them. *Tianxia* envisaged a sense of the world and not a sense of the state, as proposed by the concept of *polis*. Therefore, in China the state structure has been given to several systems, a state has been created as if it were a world (Zhao, 2022).

In the opening speech of the first "One Belt, One Road Forum for international cooperation", Xi Jinping stated that:

> The ancient Silk Road extended to the region of the Nile valley, the Tigris and the Euphrates, the Indus and the Ganges, the Yellow River and the Yangtze, linking the cradles of the Egyptian, Babylonian, Indian or Chinese civilizations, and it expanded the convergence zones of different beliefs such as Buddhism, Christianity and Islam, widening the regions inhabited by different peoples and races. Different civilizations, religions, and nationalities sought common ground by dismissing their disputes, sought openness and tolerance, and together wrote magnificent poems on mutual respect and created beautiful scroll paintings on common development.
>
> (Xi, 2017: 3)

In other words, the Belt and Road Initiative is a project that transcends relations between States, but rather incorporates the link between the multiplicity of peoples, civilizations and religions that extend throughout the world.

References

Cardilli, R. (2019). "驪靬 (Lijian/Liqian) Una città romana in Cina. Il problema giuridico del rapporto tra Impero e città 中国的古罗马城市骊靬---帝国与城市之间关系的法律问题". In R. Cardilli, L. Formichella, S. Porcelli, & Y. O. Stoeva (Coord.) (Eds.), *Chang'An e Roma Eurasia e Via Della Seta Diritto, Società, Economia* (pp. 45–59). Milano: Wolters Kluwer, CEDAM.

Caselli, G. P. (2019). "Roma, la Cina e la via della seta". In *Diritto@Storia. Rivista internazionale di Scienze Giuridiche e Tradizione Romana.* Retrieved September 20, 2022, from https://www.dirittoestoria.it/17/memorie/Caselli-Roma-Cina-via-della-seta.htm.

Chan, W. (1968a). The story of Chinese philosophy. In C. A. Moore (Ed.), *The Chinese mind: Essentials of Chinese philosophy and culture* (pp. 31–76). Honolulu: East-West Center Press, University of Hawaii Press.

Chan, W. (1968b) Chinese theory and practice, with special reference to humanism. In C. A. Moore (Ed.), *The Chinese mind: Essentials of Chinese philosophy and culture* (pp. 11–30). Honolulu: East-West Center Press, University of Hawaii Press.

Cheng, A. (2000). *Storia del pensiero cinese. Dalle origini allo "studio del mistero".* Torino: Einaudi.

Costa, P., & Zolo, D. (a cura di). (2002). *Lo Stato di diritto. Storia, teoria, critica.* Milano: Feltrinelli.

Ding, M. (2005). Introduzione al diritto cinese contemporaneo. *Diritto cinese e sistema giuridico romanistico* (pp. 101–106). Torino: Giappichelli.

Esborraz, D. (2018). L'altra Via della Seta: La rotta transpacifica del 'Galeone di Manila'(1565–1815). Aspetti storico-giuridici. *Roma e America-Diritto Romano Comune-Rivista Di Diritto Dell'integrazione e Unificazione Del Diritto in Eurasia e in America Latina, 39*, 121–144.

Grecchi, L. (2009). *L'umanesimo della antica filosofia cinese* Pistoia: Petite plaisance.

Irti, N. (2017). "La Cina verso l'unità di un Codice civilie". In *Corriere della Sera*, January 30, 2017. Available at: https://www.corriere.it/opinioni/17_gennaio_31/cina-l-unita-un-codice-civile-31b22dce-e705-11e6-b669-c1011b4a3bf2.shtml

Jiang, P. (2005a). "Il risorgere dello spirito del diritto romano in Cina". In *Diritto cinese e sistema giuridico romanistico* (pp. 49–56). Torino: Giappichelli.

Jiang, P. (2005b). "Il diritto romano nella Repubblica Popolare Cinese". In *Diritto cinese e sistema giuridico romanistico* (pp. 3–11). Torino: Giappichelli.

Jullien, F. (2011). *L'ansa e l'accesso. Strategie del senso in Cina, Grecia.* Milano-Udine: Mimesis Insegne.

Kramer, H. J. (1996). *Dialettica e definizione del Bene in Platone*. Vita e Pensiero.

Mi, J. (2005). Diritto cinese e diritto romano. *Diritto cinese e sistema giuridico romanistico* (pp. 13–27). Torino: Giappichelli.

Millward, J. A. (2013). *The silk road: A very short introduction*. Oxford: Oxford university Press.

Moore, C. A. (1968). *The Chinese mind: Essentials of Chinese philosophy and culture*. Honolulu: East- West Center Press, University of Hawaii Press.

Sen, A. (2001). Derechos Humanos y Valores Asiáticos. *Cambridge University, Anales De La Cátedra Francisco Suárez, 35*, 129–147.

Schipani, S. (2005). "Il diritto romano in Cina". In *Diritto cinese e sistema giuridico romanistico* (pp. 49–68). Torino: Giappichelli.

Schipani, S. (2009). "Diritto romano in Cina. XXI Secolo". In *Enciclopedia di Diritto romano Treccani*. Retrieved September 21, 2022, from https://www.treccani.it/enciclopedia/diritto-romano-in-cina_%28XXI-Secolo%29/.

Scarpari, M. (2019). L'umanesimo etico di Confucio. In *Religioni, spiritualità ed etica con caratteristiche cinesi*. https://www.twai.it/articles/lumanesimo-etico-di-confucio/#_ftnref3.

Sini, C. (2012). *Il sapere dei segni. Filosofia e semiotica*. Milano: Editoriale Jaca Book S.r.l.

Staiano, M. F. (2016). *Las recientes evoluciones de las relaciones entre China y Latinoamérica: el caso Argentina*. Mercosur abc.

Villagrán, I. (2019). "Dinámicas y espacios de interacción entre el mundo chino y sus periferias: política, comercio y cultura en el imperio temprano" (中华与周边交往的动力与空间: 早期王朝的政治、经贸与文化). In M. F. Staiano, L. Bogado Bordazar, & M. Caubet (Coord.) (Eds.), *China: una nueva estrategia geopolítica global (la iniciativa la Franja y la Ruta)* (pp. 14–20). Argentina: Universidad Nacional de La Plata.

Xi, J. (2017). "Let's work together to build the 'One Belt, One Road' initiative. Xi Jinping's speech at the opening ceremony of the 'One Belt, One Road' International Forum", Beijing, May 14, 2017. Retrieved October 22, 2022, from http://politica-china.org/wp-content/plugins/download-attachments/includes/download.php?id=1093.

Yan, X. (2011). *Ancient Chinese thought, modern Chinese power*. New Jersey: Princeton University Press.

Yang, Z. (2005). La tradizione filosofica del diritto romano e del diritto cinese antico. *Diritto cinese e sistema giuridico romanistico* (pp. 29–53). Torino: Giappichelli.

Zhao, T. (2022). "Tianxia 1.2", podcast by Gabriele Battaglia. Retrieved October 2, 2022, from https://www.rsi.ch/rete-due/programmi/cultura/laser/Tianxia-1.2-15662734.html?f=podcast-shows.

Zoja, L. (2007). *Giustizia e bellezza*. Torino: Bollati Boringhieri Editore.

Chapter 2
International Law as a Pioneer in the Chinese Domestic Juridical System

2.1 "Constitutive Union" Between the General Theory of Law and the International Relations Theory in China

The Chinese legal system can be described as the product of a multidimensional and cumulative cultural process, in which the various layers of modern legal innovations overlapped with those of ancient Chinese thought, generating a fluid sedimentation of concepts, schemes, models and paradigms belonging to different periods, which were sometimes fragmented (Staiano, 2016). Fragmentation and "legal flexibility" (Castellucci, 2007) is one of the main characteristics of Chinese law, as well as "legal pluralism" (Beatriz, 2015).

The 1949 marked the breaking point, or rather of evolution, between the Sinic juridical system and the Chinese juridical system (Mi, 2005: 21). Before '49 the legal system was the one formed during the Qing dynasty until the beginning of the Republic. After the inauguration of the Republic, the entire system previously created was eliminated, as a sign of feudal traditions, without however contrasting the signs of ancient tradition, steeped in the rituals of the Chinese population. From 1949 the legal evolution was slow and extremely connected with Mao's new political column and annihilated during the cultural revolution (1966–1976). It was only from 1978–1979 that Chinese law began a process of rapid development, reorganising itself from its origins but in line with the law of Western countries, especially those with Roman roots.

The element capable of explaining the reason for these Chinese characteristics (which will be explored in the next chapters) is the relationship. Indeed, China had to carry out the construction of an "emergency" legal system due to the collision with Western countries at the end of the nineteenth century. The intercultural legal dialogue between late Qing China and Western colonial powers was not very prosperous at the time. In fact, this stage is remembered as the "century of national humiliation", due to a series of "unequal treaties". The disastrous evidence of this difficult period for China, in which it was necessary to pass from a broad idea of *Tianxia* to the creation of a "Chinese nation", is undoubtedly the loss of Hong Kong and Macao,

M. F. Staiano, *Chinese Law and Its International Projection*, Understanding China,
https://doi.org/10.1007/978-981-19-9578-1_2

which have only recently returned under the Chinese sovereignty, respectively in 1997 and 1999. It is precisely in these two special administrative regions that the fusion between "Western characteristics" and the "Chinese characteristics" are most easily observed, preserving that accumulation of legal elements that highlight the pluralistic mixture of law.

Without going into a historical study, which is not the subject of this work, we can however note that already in the Confucian perspective the relationship constituted the essence of the human being, and in the same way, the relationship constituted the evolution of the nation. Chinese, which "is not a static reality but which evolves and transforms in step with its interactions with the rest of the world" (Gallelli, 2021: 35).

The term relationships in the Chinese language is defined by an expression that has a very important and profound meaning, *Guanxi* (关系). According to Confucian philosophy, in fact, it is relationships that give man prestige. The individual is relevant when he is part of a community, of family, hierarchical and friendship ties. Relationships are fundamental tools for building an individual's life and that is why they are connected with three other key concepts: *Renqing, Lian* and *Mianzi.*

Renqing (人情) expresses the feeling of humanity that is reflected in the moral obligation to maintain interpersonal relationships.[1] In line with International Relations, we can implement this principle in interstate relations. In Chinese diplomacy, it is very important to get to know each other, virtual knowledge is not enough, but it is necessary to meet personally, share time and thoughts together between work and rest. From this principle, it can be deduced how, on the one hand, the People's Republic of China has International Relations with all countries, and how, on the other hand, these relations are not all the same. The hierarchy of relations depends not only on the history of the relations, but also on the level that China gives to this relation, according to a precise scheme. The *Lian* (脸) is moral integrity, it occurs when there is adequate behaviour in the relationship, respectful of the hierarchy and the status of each person. For example, it is a serious offence to invite a person with a certain position and accompany him with a person who does not have the same rank. In diplomatic relations there are codes that are already close to this principle.

But in International Relations, China implements very different action plans according to the hierarchical and friendship value, not the political or economic implementation, that it attributes to each country. Finally, the *Mianzi* (面子), which literally means "face", is the social perception that others have about a person; then, it can be translated as the prestige that this person has managed to achieve with his life, the reputation or social value of it. The Mianzi is the result of a general evaluation

[1] The VIII World Forum for Chinese Studies, organised by the Shanghai Academy of Social Sciences on September 10 and 11, 2019, was closed with a *lectio magistralis* by Tu Weiming, Professor Emeritus of Harvard University. After nearly 400 papers presented by researchers from around the world, talking about economics, international relations, politics, the Belt and Road Initiative and its implications in each region and globally, the rise of China, international geopolitics, etc., Prof. Tu chose to close this world event, held in the financial centre of Shanghai, with a conference on "benevolence as a universal value" (Tu, 2019). His intervention has put a firm point to all the debates of the Forum: the Rénqíng (人情) as the beginning and end of man's action at a global level, in all civilizations.

of a person, or of a State. Based on this, it is possible to understand how and why the PRC acts in very different ways in International Relations in different areas. *Mianzi* is associated with key concepts such as: "loose face", lose respect for the community 丢面子 (*Diu mianzi*); "to concede face", to give someone a chance to regain lost honor 留面子 (*Liu mianzi*); "show your face", show respect for someone, 给面子 (*Gei mianzi*).

All these concepts constantly influence the International Relations of the PRC: China evaluates and reacts with the countries in line with these values. Relations for the PRC are not transitory and brief, but strong and long-term ties and these relations have influenced the Chinese legal system from the beginning of the construction of a Chinese law.

According to Sandro Schipani, "we can identify as the date of the beginning of China's attention to the law of Western countries in 1902, when the jurists Shen Jiaben and Wu Tingfang were invited to England, North America, Spain and Peru to meet the rights of these countries" (Schipani, 2005: XII). It is therefore necessary to consider that it is precisely the scientific dialogue with these legal models that influenced China's choice of a *Civil law* legal system, discarding that of *Common law*.

2.2 The Issues of International Agreements on Human Rights as a Fundamental Step in Building the Chinese Law System

According to Liu Huawen, "the rule of law is one of the main objectives of government strategies" and "the rule of law and human rights are two interactive dimensions of China's social development" (Liu, 2010). Furthermore, "the progressive approach to international human rights law has pioneered the development of Chinese domestic law, which functions as a "tool of legal culture" (Liu, 2010). In fact, according to Liu, "Human rights law and concepts have their own humanistic and moral foundations; therefore, they produce not only general legal obligations but also humanitarian repercussions on public opinion and the moral evaluation of their implementation process, so their importance goes beyond the legal sense. In this regard, Orientals tend to add an internal moral obligation to the legal obligation" (Liu, 2010: 6).

We consider that human rights are a particular *species* of rights, as they are characterised by specific elements universally recognized first through international customs, i.e. behaviours generally recognized by the international community as binding, and subsequently codified in numerous international conventions signed and ratified by the states they adhere to. Furthermore, human rights are unavailable, inalienable, inviolable and applicable *erga omnes* as mandatory norms, i.e. *jus cogens*. This superiority of human rights over other legal categories derives from human nature itself and has been implemented on a general level by the 1969 Vienna Convention on the Law of Treaties which codifies the functioning of international law. In fact, according to the Article 53 of the Vienna Convention on the law of treaties, the mandatory norms of international law (including the rights of *jus cogens*) cannot be contradicted by international treaties, which, consequently, are null, i.e. devoid of legal effect. Again according to Article 53, "a peremptory norm of general international law is a norm accepted and recognized by the international community of States as a whole as a norm from which no derogation is permitted and which can be modified only by a subsequent norm of general international law having the same character". For this reason, human rights constitute a bridge between nations, as a "common minimum" to be taken into consideration when defining the cornerstones of a legal system.

Therefore, the evolution of human rights in China as a pioneering element of its domestic law has a double meaning: on the one hand, it constitutes an aspect of relationship with the international community; on the other, an elevation of its legal system towards an improvement of its rule of law. In fact, international human rights treaties constitute an essential pillar in the construction of the rule of law. Human rights, through customs subsequently perfected in specific conventions and implementation protocols, define a nucleus of essential principles that guide the internal legislation of the individual states which each implement them according to their own characteristics, expressed in the Constitution.

However, the path of human rights in China has not been easy because it has always been a subject sensitive to exploitation and a certain diplomacy of interference in the internal affairs of other states, generating political pressure and sometimes relations of force. In particular, until the 1980s the expression "human rights" was considered as a symbol of Western capitalism with a strong ideological sense (Liu, 2010). In this sense, it was a "prohibited expression" (Guo & Tao, 1999) replaced by other words, such as "rights", "rights and interests", "citizenship rights", even in the early 1980s when China actually began signing and ratifying human rights treaties. "Generally speaking, human rights research in China began in the late 1980s and gradually deepened. Now, with the rapid development of research and awareness of the issue, the term "human rights" has become popular in China" (Liu, 2010).

Currently, the People's Republic of China has signed the fundamental international treaties on human rights (Table 2.1) but, as observed by Liu Huawen, all Chinese domestic legislation is developing according to a strict qualitative evolution, in line with international treaties, although not yet signed or ratified by China.

> Both foreign law and international law can reflect international experience and the achievements of legal civilization, while international law is more likely to reflect universally accepted legal principles or rules, and has special significance for absorption and reference. China attaches importance to the domestic implementation of international treaties ratified or acceded to by the country, and to the implementation of general international law and various rules of international law with corresponding legal effect on China, while international treaties to which China is not a party or other rules of international law that do not have legal effect may still have reference value on legal culture.
>
> (Liu, 2020)

A clear sign of this practice are the National Human Rights Institution (NHRI), the National Human Rights Action Plan and the *White Papers* that the State Council

Table 2.1 *Source* UN treaty body database

Country	Treaty description	Treaty name	Signature date	Ratification date, accession (a), succession (d) date
China	Convention against Torture and Other Cruel Inhuman or Degrading Treatment or Punishment	CAT	12 Dec 1986	04 Oct 1988
China	Optional Protocol of the Convention against Torture	CAT-OP		
China	International Covenant on Civil and Political Rights	CCPR	05 Oct 1998	
China	Second Optional Protocol to the International Covenant on Civil and Political Rights aiming to the abolition of the death penalty	CCPR-OP2-DP		
China	Convention for the Protection of All Persons from Enforced Disappearance	CED		
China	Interstate communication procedure under the International Convention for the Protection of All Persons from Enforced Disappearance	CED, Article 32		
China	Convention on the Elimination of All Forms of Discrimination against Women	CEDAW	17 Jul 1980	04 Nov 1980
China	International Convention on the Elimination of All Forms of Racial Discrimination	CERD		29 Dec 1981 (a)
China	International Covenant on Economic, Social and Cultural Rights	CESCR	27 Oct 1997	27 Mar 2001

(continued)

Table 2.1 (continued)

Country	Treaty description	Treaty name	Signature date	Ratification date, accession (a), succession (d) date
China	International Convention on the Protection of the Rights of All Migrant Workers and Members of Their Families	CMW		
China	Convention on the Rights of the Child	CRC	29 Aug 1990	02 Mar 1992
China	Optional Protocol to the Convention on the Rights of the Child on the involvement of children in armed conflict	CRC-OP-AC	15 Mar 2001	20 Feb 2008
China	Optional Protocol to the Convention on the Rights of the Child on the sale of children child prostitution and child pornography	CRC-OP-SC	06 Sep 2000	03 Dec 2002
China	Convention on the Rights of Persons with Disabilities	CRPD	30 Mar 2007	01 Aug 2008

periodically publishes on the subject of human rights. At least since 1991, the State Council has begun a series of White Papers, although for relations with the West the most relevant are from 2011, when the White Paper on Peaceful Development was presented, and subsequently a series of White Papers on Progress and Protection of Human Rights in China (2012, 2013, 2014, 2015, 2016, 2017, 2018, 2019, 2020, 2021, 2022) and on specific topics, such as the Women's cause, persons with disabilities, poverty, ethnic groups. Furthermore, after the individuation of Chinese characteristics, White Papers started to be on the Chinese five-plan on Human Rights, on Democracy, New Era, among others.[2]

In the White Paper "The Communist Party of China and Human Rights Protection—A 100-Year Quest" of June 24, 2021[3] Chapter VII proposes "Adding diversity to the concept of human rights". Here it is affirmed that for China, there are no models ready to copy in the respect, protection and development of human rights. China must start from its prevailing realities and go its own way. By applying the

[2] For the full list of White Papers of China, visit the webpage https://english.www.gov.cn/archive/whitepaper/page_1.html.

[3] PRC State Council, white paper titled "The Communist Party of China and Human Rights Protection—A 100-Year Quest.", June 24, 2021. Available at: http://english.www.gov.cn/news/topnews/202106/24/content_WS60d41f65c6d0df57f98dbcfe.html.

principle of universality of human rights to China's national conditions, the CCP has broken new ground in protecting human rights and added diversity to the concept of human rights with its own practices. It also marks the "Promotion of human rights through development", underlining the adoption of a people-centred approach to human rights: "living a happy life is the primary human right, giving a new meaning to China's progress." in terms of human rights in the new era". It is understood the position of the people and the essential elements of the development of human rights in China, as a constant cause. In the chapter "Aiming for the comprehensive development of the people" it is stated that comprehensive development is an objective of the people in their search for a modern and strong socialist country under the leadership of the CPC, and the ultimate goal of the cause of human rights in China. There must be a coordinated development of civil, political and economic, social and cultural rights; to the coordination of the economy, society, resources and the protection of the environment, and to sustainable development for the well-being of people now and in the future. All these contents are also affirmed at an international level, proposing to Build a global community with a shared future.

In the White Paper "Moderate Prosperity in All Respects: Another Milestone Achieved in China's Human Rights" of August 2021,[4] particular emphasis is placed on the issue of poverty and more balanced development to promote moderate prosperity and promote human rights, putting an end to extreme poverty and guaranteeing the right to a standard of living. Likewise, it is proposed to promote human rights with the development and guarantee of economic, social and cultural rights, as well as civil and political rights with laws and governance.

The White Papers reveal China's need to systematise the matters in which domestic legislation is processed in order to then project it internationally, as in a sort of juridical osmosis. They have developed as a necessary practice of external communication of the internal and international actions promoted by the Chinese Government and propose a Chinese reinterpretation of essential lemmas on the subject of international relations, international law and human rights. The need to propose a "Chinese way" in terms of law and, in particular, human rights, is a necessary strategy for progressively adapting domestic law to international human rights law, which emanates from another epistemological matrix, that of Western liberal rights. The dichotomy, however, is merely apparent because an absolute dogma does not exist, and never has existed, an archetype of the rule of law valid for all (Staiano, 2016), therefore what must be scientifically taken into account is the progressive adaptation of the law Chinese internal law to international law, through a necessary internalisation, in line with the principle of hierarchy of internal sources.

[4] PRC State Council, white paper titled "Moderate Prosperity in All Respects: Another Milestone Achieved in China's Human Rights.", August 10th, 2021. Available at: http://english.www.gov.cn/archive/whitepaper/202108/12/content_WS611492b4c6d0df57f98de5ac.html.

2.3 The Development of Chinese Domestic Law in the Light of International Agreements on Human Rights

Chinese legislation has imposed an essential corollary to the construction of a socialist state of law through the constitutional reform of March 14, 2004, which introduced in article 33: "The state protects and guarantees human rights". This article represents the need for China to hook the rule of law to fundamental rights, with an approach increasingly marking China's transition to a "constitutional rule of law," perhaps because all foreign observers look to the socialist state of law as unable to implement all the typical structures of the rule of law systems, especially in the matter of separation of powers and *Check and Balances* (Supiot; Granet; Castellucci; Beatriz; Ajani). Likewise, human rights represent significant data as one of the goals of the rule of law (Liu, 2010).

Some examples can clarify the extent of the profound legal evolution achieved thanks to the internal adaptation of international conventions on fundamental rights.

(a) **Women's rights**

The first human rights convention signed and ratified by China is the Convention against all forms of discrimination against women (CEDAW): China has been a party to the Convention against All Forms of Discrimination against Women since November 4, 1980. Despite not having ratified the Optional Protocol, the People's Republic of China is a party to the Convention and is therefore bound to submit every four years to the Secretary-General a report on the legislative, judicial, administrative or other measures it has taken to give effect to the provisions of the Convention, the progress made, possibly indicating the factors and difficulties affecting the conditions of application of the obligations set forth in the Convention.

The White Paper on Gender Equality and Women's Development in China issued by the State Council on September 22, 2015, points out a large number of legislative changes in line with the gender mainstreaming approach, which have generated an advance in health, education, work, political inclusion, personal development implemented by ad hoc laws, and the economy.[5]

"China represents the spirit and principles of the Convention on the Elimination of All Forms of Discrimination against Women (CEDAW) in making its laws, policies and plans, makes unremitting efforts to eliminate all forms of discrimination against women, safeguard the rights and interests of women in accordance with the law, and promote gender equality".[6]

Subsequently, the State Council Information Office of the People's Republic of China on September 19, 2019 published a white paper titled "Equality, Development

---

[5] PRC State Council, *White Paper on Gender Equality and Women's Development in China* http://english.gov.cn/archive/white_paper/2015/09/22/content_281475195668448.htm.

[6] PRC State Council, *White Paper on Gender Equality and Women's Development in China,* cit.

and Sharing: Progress of Women's Cause in 70 Years Since New China's Founding."[7] Since the first chapter, it is reiterated as "Boosting the comprehensive development of women and achieving gender equality have been perceived as important components of the socialism system with Chinese characteristics. China has always attached great importance to such development and equality." The notions of development and equality appear to be linked by the profound awareness that gender equality is not simply a "formal" datum, but concrete, constant and co-essential to the development of the whole society, in line with the principle of substantial equality established in the 'Article 48 of the Constitution of the People's Republic of China: "Women in the People's Republic of China enjoy equal rights with men in all spheres of life, political, economic, cultural and social, and family life. The state protects the rights and interests of women, applies the principle of equal pay for equal work for men and women alike and trains and selects cadres from among women". The chapters of the White Paper reflect the efforts undertaken by the Chinese Government (Table 2.2) to decisively improve women's rights and, therefore, the development of all Chinese society.

In addition, China has supported a promotion of gender equality in a regional perspective: it has launched a project to improve the capacity to deal with gender issues and achieve the United Nations Millennium Development Goals in the region. for Asia and the Pacific, at the Economic and Social Commission for Asia and the Pacific (ESCAP); has organised the Forum on Women and the Economy in the Asia-Pacific Economic Cooperation (APEC) in 2014; has hosted the East Asia Ministerial Meeting on Gender Equality, within the framework of the ASEAN cooperation mechanism plus China, Japan and South Korea ("10 + 3").[8] Recently, on November 11, 2022, the 25th China-ASEAN Summit took place in Phnom Penh. The final China-ASEAN Joint Statement on Strengthening Common and Sustainable Development contains several refers to the gender equality, especially at point 7 on "Implement the agreed deliverables of the China-ASEAN Year of Digital Economy Cooperation", with particular regard to "promote women's entrepreneurship"; and at point 12 on "Promote women's role in the implementation of the ACRF for sustainable development and growth and socio-economic resilience in the region".[9]

The approval of the Convention on the Elimination of all Forms of Discrimination against Women, approved by the General Assembly on December 18, 1979 and entered into force on September 3, 1981, has undoubtedly represented the most important international act in the matter of gender equality. This Convention codifies all previous instruments related to human rights in general and the human rights

---

[7] PRC State Council, *Equality, Development and Sharing: Progress of Women's Cause in 70 Years Since New China's Founding,* available at https://english.www.gov.cn/archive/whitepaper/201909/20/content_WS5d843344c6d0bcf8c4c13ba7.html.

[8] PRC State Council, *White Paper on Gender Equality and Women's Development in China,* cit.

[9] China-ASEAN Joint Statement on Strengthening Common and Sustainable Development, 2022, available at http://english.www.gov.cn/premier/news/202211/12/content_WS636edc8bc6d0a757729e2f10.html.

Table 2.2 *Source* White paper equality, development and sharing: progress of women's cause in 70 years since new China's founding (2019)

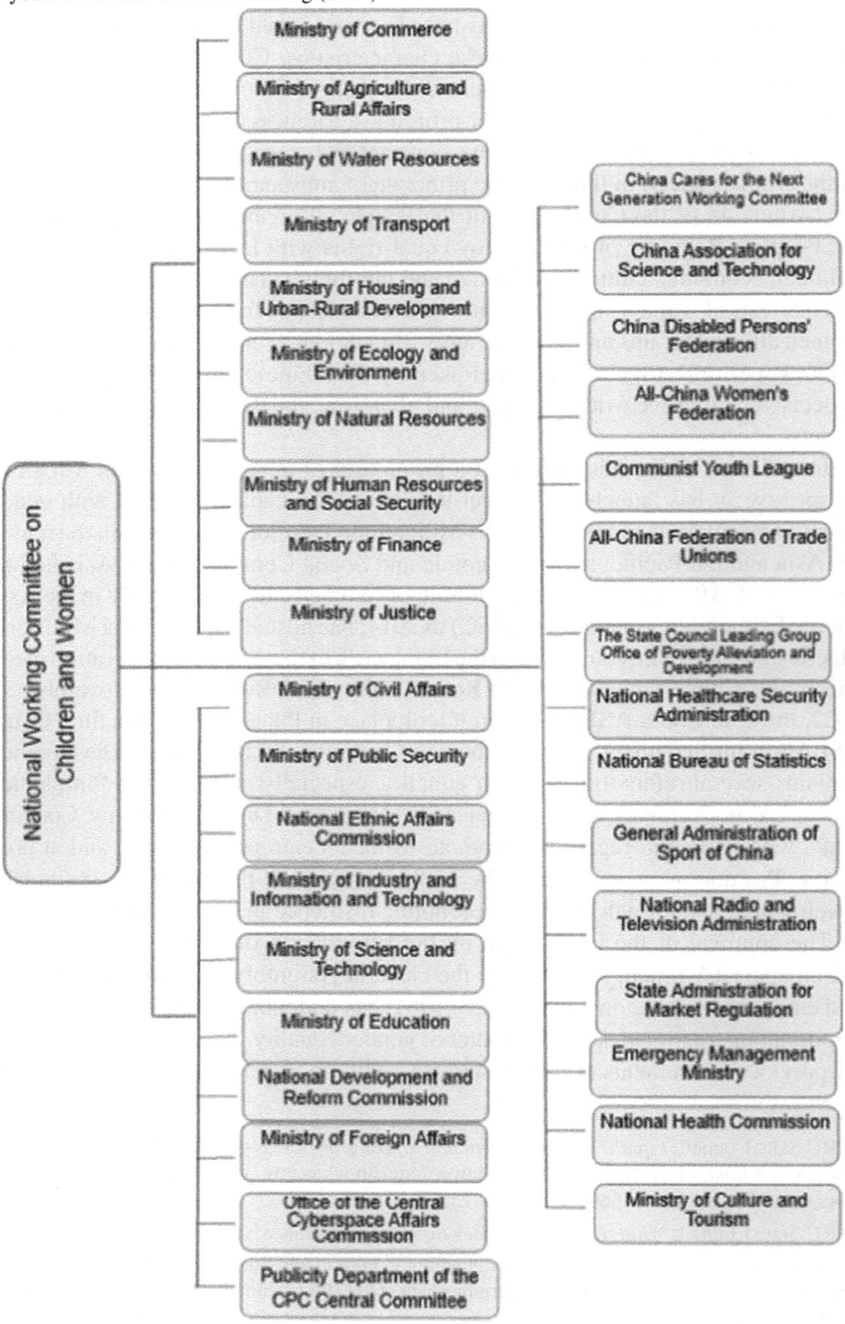

of women in particular. Until then, many in the international community relegated violence against women to the "private" sphere. The Convention went beyond this point of view, taking into account all forms of violence, including domestic violence, as violations of human rights, which makes them susceptible to the responsibilities of States and the international community. Therefore, this tool provides a valid guarantee for gender equality and freedom from all forms of discrimination by States and private agents. The elimination of discrimination is required in all areas of human existence, without distinction. The definition of discrimination provided by CEDAW is: "For the purposes of the [...] Convention, the term discrimination against women shall denote any distinction, exclusion or restriction based on sex that is intended or has the effect of impairing or annul the recognition, enjoyment or exercise by women, regardless of their marital status, on the basis of the equality of men and women, of human rights and fundamental freedoms in the political, economic, social, cultural and civil fields or in any other".[10]

The rights contained in the Convention can be classified into three different categories, depending on the type of actions required by the State: (a) a first group of norms grants a specific right, focused on civil and political rights; (b) other norms require the State to adopt appropriate measures, for example, in order to change discriminatory patterns and behaviour patterns; (c) Other rules require the Member States to implement actions aimed at achieving a specific goal, in particular towards respect for economic and social rights. The peculiar character of the Convention is represented by the desire to reconcile the mere recognition of the right to enjoy equal treatment with respect to men, providing a clear obligation of States to adopt positive measures that, as an exception to the principle of equality formal, enable them to pursue the objective of equality of women with men, in terms of effectiveness.

We can include among the domestic laws of the People's Republic of China in line with these positive obligations for the member states of CEDAW: the reform of the law on marriage, the reform and phasing out of the law on population and family planning, the contract law for rural land and the law on the protection of women's rights and interests, as well as promulgating more than 100 regulations on the protection of women's rights and interests (Liu, 2010). The Civil Code, the first law to carry the title "code" in New China, which took effect on January 1, 2021, emphasises the protection of women's rights and interests in marriage and family. The Anti-Domestic Violence Law of the People's Republic of China, which took effect on March 1, 2016, protects women's personal rights in the family. The Family Education Promotion Law of the People's Republic of China, which took effect on January 1, 2022, makes clear that the State, schools and society provide guidance on and support and services for family education. The Law on Rural Land Contracts of the People's Republic of China was amended in 2018 to improve the legal basis for

[10] UN, *Convention on the Elimination of All Forms of Discrimination Against Women*, Article 1, available at http://www.un.org/womenwatch/daw/cedaw/text/econvention.htm.

protecting rural women's land rights and interests. Gender-equality-evaluation mechanisms have been established—at the national level and in 31 provinces, autonomous regions or municipalities—to reinforce the legal protection of women's rights and interests.

The action of the All China Women's Federation (Table 2.3) was fundamental in this profound juridical-cultural evolution in application of the gender mainstream, which has guided, through constant studies of the intersectionality of gender-based discrimination and violence, pilot projects for the improvement the conditions of girls and women, in order to guarantee them high levels of education and participation in the socio-economic and cultural development of the country, promoting an integral development of the person in conditions of equality with man.

Table 2.3 *Source* White paper equality, development and sharing: progress of women's cause in 70 years since new China's founding (2019)

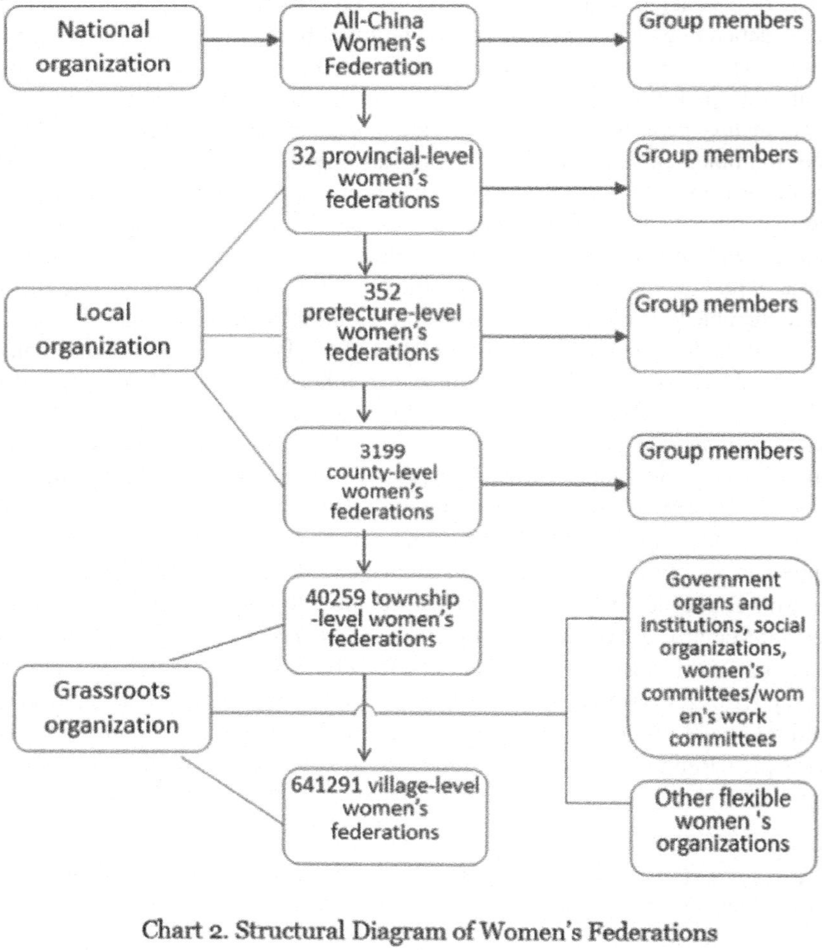

(b) **People with disabilities' rights**

China has ratified the Convention on the Rights of Persons with Disabilities (CRPD) on August 1, 2008 and has not signed the Convention's Optional Protocol, which provides for the competence of the Committee to receive and consider communications from individuals or groups of individuals who claim to be victims of violations of the provisions of the Convention by a State Party.

In this case, the Law of the People's Republic of China on the Protection of Persons with Disabilities is prior to the ratification of the CRPD, as soon as it was approved on December 28, 1990,[11] during the 17th meeting of the Standing Committee of the plenary session of the Seventh National People's Assembly. However, following the enforcement of the CRPD the 1990 law was profoundly amended in 2008,[12] in order to improve the right to work and study for people with disabilities. Finally, still considered insufficient with respect to the specific cases that have arisen in China over the years, it was issued a new Law of October 26, 2012, in force from May 1, 2013,[13] with which forced hospitalisation in psychiatric hospitals in the absence of the patient's consent was finally prohibited. Furthermore, an ad hoc Committee has been set up for the evaluation of the cases of hospitalisation necessary for the seriously ill or who may harm themselves or others.

Since the 1990 Law, it is interesting to note how the definition of "disability" provided by Article 2 coincides exactly with the classifications prepared by the World Health Organization (WHO), effectively aligning itself with the international scientific debate existing on the matter internationally. The 2008 reform envisaged a further articulation of the objectives of the law, providing for interventions increasingly in line with a "disability perspective" in rehabilitation, education, employment, cultural life, social security, accessible environment and legal liability. The legislative structure that has supported and improved the rights of people with disabilities is very advanced, as the system provides for the protection of every aspect of the disabled person's life: The Regulations on the Education of Persons with Disabilities (1994); The Rules on the Employment of Disabled Persons (2007); The Employment Promotion Law (2007); The 12th Five Year National Programme on Disability (2011–2015); The Regulations on Construction of Accessible Environment (2012); The Mental Health Law (2012, into force in 2013). All these laws contributed to realisation of Decent Work Country Programmes in China (2006–2010), addressing the

---

[11] *Zhonhua Renmin Gongheguo Canjiren Baozhang Fa* 中华人民共和国残疾人保障法 (Law of the People's Republic of China on Protection of Disabled Persons), 1990, avaible at http://www.gov.cn/jrzg/2008-04/24/content_953439.htm.

[12] *Zhonhua Renmin Gongheguo Canjiren Baozhang Fa* 中华人民共和国残疾人保障法 (Law of the People's Republic of China on Protection of Disabled Persons), 2008, available at http://www.npc.gov.cn/zgrdw/englishnpc/Law/2011-02/14/content_1620414.htm.

[13] *Zhonghua Renmin Gongheguo Jingshen Weisheng Fa* 中华人民共和国精神卫生法 (2012年10月26日第十一届全国人民代表大会常务委员会第二十九次会议通过) Mental Health Law of the People's Republic of China (Adopted at the 29th Standing Committee Meeting of the 11th National People's Congress on October 26, 2012, into force from May 1st 2013), available at http://www.gov.cn/jrzg/2012-10/26/content_2252122.htm.

needs of those most disadvantaged in the labour market, including disabled persons, and promoting worker rights and fundamental principles and labour rights at work.[14]

As well as for Women rights, also in the protection of people with disabilities' rights there is the China Disabled Persons' Federation (CDPF), founded in 1988 and several organisations for people with disabilities, of people with disabilities and Ngo. The most relevant element in affirming rights on people with disabilities in China was the permanent efforts of sensibilization by these organisations, because disability still represents a strong stigmatisation in social life, so their action was fundamental to build a common consciousness on the topic. The application of the legal evolution, like the scientific one, in terms of disabled people has been made possible at a social level through the "socialisation" of the meaning of disability. This is why the Mental Health Law, which came into force on 1 May 2013, had a very strong impact. This law provides for the treatment of the mentally disabled with care and attention for the rehabilitation of patients, through a series of containment actions pathologies with playful, recreational, educational and work activities, and with the permanent intermediation of families as well as medical personnel (Articles 3 and 6). The essential element is the recognition of the personal dignity, personal and financial safety of people with mental disorders (Article 4), as the mentally disabled must be protected and respected by the whole of society (Article 5).

The "social responsibility" of disability, in terms of containment and direction towards social rehabilitation is a recent issue in China.

The State Council Information Office on July 25 issued a white paper on the country's efforts to protect rights and interests of persons with disabilities over the past 70 years, titled "Equality, Participation and Sharing: 70 Years of Protecting the Rights and Interests of Persons with Disabilities in the PRC". Besides a preamble and a conclusion, the white paper consisted of ten sections: "Development of the Cause of Persons with Disabilities", "Mechanisms for the Protection of Rights and Interests of Persons with Disabilities", "Health and Rehabilitation", "Special Education and Inclusive Education", "Employment and Entrepreneurship", "Basic Life and Social Security", "Creating an Accessible Environment and Enabling Mobility", "Personal Freedom and Non-Discrimination", "Creating a Good Social Environment", and "International Exchanges and Cooperation." By April 2018, more than 80 laws and 50 administrative regulations had been passed concerning the protection of the rights and interests of persons with disabilities. Recently, in March 2022, a further white paper on the social inclusion of people with disabilities through sport was issued: "China's Parasports: Progress and the Protection of Rights". In the Preamble it is clear the link between sport inclusion and the improvement of people with disabilities' rights: "Sports are important for all individuals, including those with a disability. Developing parasports is an effective way to help persons with disabilities to improve physical fitness, pursue physical and mental rehabilitation, participate in social activities, and achieve all-round development. It also provides a special opportunity for the public to better understand the potential and value of the disabled, and promote social harmony and progress. In addition, developing parasports is of great importance in

[14] ILO, *Inclusion of People with Disabilities in China,* January 2013.

ensuring that persons with disabilities can enjoy equal rights, integrate readily into society, and share the fruits of economic and social progress. Participation in sports is an important right of persons with disabilities as well as an integral component of human rights protection.[15]"

There are many experiences of international cooperation in terms of improving the social conditions of people with disabilities, and the role of civil society in the juridical-cultural advancement of these sensitive matters has been substantial, as previously stated. "A greater participation of civil society" constitutes, indeed, a "New trend regarding Human Rights" (Liu, 2010) and in line with a progressive internalisation of the multiple manifestations and affirmations of human rights in China. In this sense, we can state that the principle of legal effectiveness, i.e. the awareness of the law through behaviour systematically aligned with the regulatory provisions by the population, in terms of human rights in China is gradually being implemented in line with international provisions.

References

Castellucci, I. (2007). Rule of law with Chinese characteristics. *Annual Survey of International and Comparative Law, 13*, 35–92.

Gallelli, B. (2021). *La Cina di oggi in otto parole*. Bologna: Mulino.

Guo, D., & Tao, L. (1999). "How the forbidden zone of human rights was broken through". In *Jurisprudence, Chinese journal of the east college of political science and law* (issue 5). Shanghai, China.

Juárez Aguilar, B. (2015). "¿Estado de derecho liberal o socialista? Perspectivas desde la teoría socialista y del Partido Comunista de China". In *5° Simposio Electrónico Internacional sobre Política China.*

Liu, H. (2010). "Los Derechos Humanos en China, en el marco del Derecho Internacional". In *Revista del Instituto de Estudios Jurídicos de la Universidad Nacional Autónoma de México (UNAM).*

Liu, H. (2020). "Lun Xi Jinping fazhi sixiang zhong de guoji fa yaoyi" ("On the essentials of international law in Xi Jinping's thought of rule of law"). *Bijiao Fa Yanjiu (Comparative Law Studies), 6*, 1–13.

Mi, J. (2005). Diritto cinese e diritto romano. *Diritto cinese e sistema giuridico romanistico* (pp. 13–27). Torino: Giappichelli.

Schipani, S. (2005). "Breve nota". In *Diritto cinese e sistema giuridico romanistico* (pp. IX–XVI). Torino: Giappichelli.

Staiano, M. F. (2016). *Las recientes evoluciones de las relaciones entre China y Latinoamérica: el caso Argentina.* Mercosur abc.

Tu, W. (2019). *Lectio Magistralis* "The Benevolence as Universal Principle" in the *VIII World Forum on China Studies. China and the World: Progressing Together over 70 Years*, organized by Shanghai Social Sciences Academy. The Oriental Riverside Hotel - Intercontinental Shanghai Pudong, Shanghai, September 11, 2019.

[15] PRC State Council, *White Paper on China's Parasports: Progress and the Protection of Rights*, March 2, 2022, available at https://english.www.gov.cn/archive/whitepaper/202203/03/content_WS62206416c6d09c94e48a5d84.html.

Chapter 3
The Evolution of the Chinese Legal System: Building a "Rule of Law" with Chinese Characteristics

The modernization of the socialist rule-of-law state with Chinese characteristics is essentially defined by the use of the law as an instrument of institutional legitimacy. Therefore, the affirmation of the rule of law in China was not an immediate step, above all if we consider on the one hand the insurmountable difficulty of providing a clear definition of "rule of law", and on the other if we want to consider valid the claim that in China there is a certain cultural "resistance" to the law due to the traditional importance of rituals (*Li*).[1]

Under the first profile, in fact, we must recognize the ambiguity and variability of the concept of the rule of law, as a precious intellectual experimentation against absolutism and the tyranny of autarkic governments throughout history, but imperfect as a human product. To think that the rule of law was born in the West in an absolute sense without an ethical, political and social orientation, where the force of the restrictive law of power is perfect, with impeccable implementation of the principle of legality, is a methodological error that we have to consider when analysing the Chinese system. On the other hand, a certain vocation to "violence" in the concept of Greek-Roman law, explained in its modern corporality by Foucault, is common to that of the *Fa* of the Legists. The same function of law is put under discussion today, being surpassed by the technique of capitalism (Severino, 2010). With reference to the State, we can speak of the Western democratic experience as a scheme in deep crisis regarding the legitimacy of power and the mechanisms for creating consensus (Habermas, 2016). So, as Max Weber warned us, our freedom is threatened with being suffocated by an "iron cage" (Weber, 1991), that is, the authoritarian oppression that comes from both capitalism and other forms of power based purely on teleological efficiency, rational calculation and control.

Under the second profile, we must think that the uniqueness of the rule of law in China is embodied not so much in the sources of law, or in the modifications and inventions that the Chinese legislator has developed, but in its pre-legal autopoietic system, focused on a certain "unbearability of any form of coercion, which defines

[1] See Chap. 1.

M. F. Staiano, *Chinese Law and Its International Projection*, Understanding China,
https://doi.org/10.1007/978-981-19-9578-1_3

Chinese customs through the formula: Neither God nor Law" (Granet, 1988: 475–476). In this sense, it must be recognized that the social change of the Chinese population, compared to Granet's description, has been substantial, and it is for this reason that we must analyse the constant process of legal cultural evolution of Chinese society which is marking a new legal epistemology, in line with the new era.

3.1 Building a System of Socialist Rule of Law with Chinese Characteristics

With reference to the rule of law in contemporary China, it can be mentioned how in 1997, during the XV National Congress of the PCC, *fazhi* was spoken of as a "basic strategy" to be developed to achieve the objective of "building a socialist country governed by the law". This represents, then, the means chosen and used towards socialist modernization. It can be deduced that this year marks a new stage of transition towards the legalisation of the PRC: the strategy implemented was represented by Law, a tool that, although it existed in Chinese culture, was not developed in common with foreign traditions. Those practices born as pilot experiments in the Exclusive Economic Zones inaugurated by Deng Xiaoping in 1978 to dialogue with foreign companies, now became an internal structural necessity, a method of social stability, of internal development through an internalisation of external standards with a contemporary internationalisation of China in the world.

After this Congress, in 1999, the Constitution was amended, including paragraph 1 in Article 5: "The PRC governs the country according to law and with the intention of building a legal socialist country." However, for the PRC the implementation of the *fazhi* does not represent just an icon, but the beginning of a long process (Li, 2008). In fact, at the XVI Congress of the PCC in 2002, the objectives focused on: (a) improving socialist democracy and the legal system; (b) govern the country through law; (c) create a moderately prosperous society. Important reforms of the Constitution followed, especially in Article 33 in which it is established that "The State respects and guarantees human rights." Respect for human rights is the key corollary to the concept of the rule of law, which in each legal tradition has represented the limit that the State has in relation to citizens: a clear sign of the need for the PRC to be recognized as an interlocutor that respects the same canons as the other members of the international community. So strong is this new impulse for reform that in the XVII Congress of the PCC in 2007, the acceleration of the construction of a socialist country under a rule of law was imposed. Finally, in 2010, this task was associated with building a socialist legal system with Chinese characteristics. This specification of the *fazhi* with Chinese characteristics has been highlighted to involve some typical elements of the Chinese system with the country's new economic and social trends. In fact, the economy is thought of as a necessary basis for legal construction (Economic Constitution), as it had been described in the primary stage of socialism, which had the purpose of enriching the system with different Chinese characteristics.

In this sense, it is worth highlighting the principle of the new normality, which implies the importance of the transition of the economy from high-speed growth to medium-high speed growth, towards an improvement in environmental conditions and quality of the lives of citizens, in search of less internal contradiction, not only in environmental terms but also in terms of inequality. This axis is one of the four integral tasks of the new general policy of the PRC provided by Xi Jinping in March 2015. These four principles are: building a moderately prosperous society; strengthening reforms; the government of the nation in accordance with the law (Rule of Law); rigid Party control (war on corruption).

In these years, the evolution of the process of proposing and implementing the law as a government strategy has taken place: it can be affirmed then that the legal system has coincided with the economic development and social progress of the country, because it has granted legal guarantees for the scientific advancement and harmonious and peaceful development. The legal system is characterised by a "vertical" structure, that is, state power represents the fundamental element and the production of legal norms is based on state legislation. However, beyond this centralised normative power, there is another typology of norms that does not belong to a state production, but rather has a "social" matrix, customary law. So, it can be affirmed that on a formal side, Chinese law is constituted by a complete systemic construction; but, on the application side, there is a certain distance between the reality of social life and that provided by official law, since in some areas social law seemed to work better in relationships between individuals. This follows that tradition of legal culture that has not allowed an immediate implementation of the laws in China as a *tabula rasa*, Chinese society being a culture inspired by deep traditions. From this point of view, however, in China in recent times, "legal modernism" and the vision of state law as the most powerful source are being criticised, seeking cooperation between it and social law. This is not to underestimate the importance of the law as an instrument of social control, but to emphasise that it is necessary to use different, more flexible systems as well. In fact, there are some "indirect" sources of Law, which are the policies and directives of the Communist Party. The jurisdictional source is also becoming a more important source, especially in matters that still do not have precise regulations.

Within this framework, on March 15, 2000, the Law on Legislation[2] which, in accordance with the principles established by the 1982 Constitution, establishes for the first time the hierarchy and competence of the written sources of Law, contributing to order this matter in formal terms. The Chinese legal system is based on 3 levels (Laws, Administrative Regulations, Local Regulations, with the Constitution as the backbone) and 7 areas: Civil Law, Commercial Law, Economic Law, Social Law, Criminal Law, Litigious Procedure, Non-litigious Procedure. The legislative system in China is structured in the following laws and regulations: (a) The Constitution; (b) The Law (the fundamental legal norms approved by the National People's Assembly

---

[2] Law on Legislation (*Zhonghua renmin gongheguo lifa fa*), approved on March 15, 2000 by the Third Session of the Ninth National People's Congress, promulgated by Order of the President of the People's Republic of China no. 31 of March 15, 2000, in force since July 1, 2000.

and the other laws adopted by the Standing Committee); (c) The administrative regulations adopted by the State Council; (d) The local regulations adopted by the popular assemblies and the provincial permanent committees and other corresponding levels; (e) The regulations and standards adopted by the secretariats and special committees; (f) The regulations and norms adopted by the provincial local governments and other corresponding levels; (g) Autonomous regulations and special regulations adopted by the people's congresses of the national autonomous regions, prefectures and counties ratified by the standing committees of the people's congresses at a higher level; (h) The military regulations and norms adopted by the Central Military Committee; (i) The International Treaties and Agreements ratified by the Standing Committee of the APN and the Council of State; (j) Authorised legislation delegated by the APN, the Standing Committee and the State Council (Jihong, 2008). National Laws are the norms created by the People's Assembly and its Permanent Committee, and have the value of framework laws that establish universal general principles that each administrative level has to fill according to its needs and characteristics. The Regulations are the rules, with the force of law, created by administrative or judicial bodies and by local governments at all levels: (a) Regulations of the Council of State and its Ministries (Administrative Regulations); (b) Laws and Regulations of the local authorities (by the local People's Assemblies); (c) Local or Autonomous Region regulations. It is therefore necessary to know the administrative levels of the PRC to be able to monitor the Regulations in each area. In China there are: 23 Provinces, 5 Autonomous Regions, 4 Municipalities directly administered by the Central Government (Article 30 Const.), 2 Special Administrative Regions (Article 31 Const.) governed by the principle "One Country, two systems" (Fig. 3.1).

To these divisions are added the administrative distinctions of the territory, and the legal peculiarities of the Special Economic Zones, the Free Trade Zones, as well as some economic development programs implemented by the government in certain areas (Figs. 3.2, 3.3, 3.4 and Table 3.1). This legal fragmentation of China, which has been described as "variable geometries" (Castellucci, 2012), is the result of an overlapping of unique historical and political experiences, which has intersected with Western elements, especially after the reform policy and opening of Deng Xiaoping. However, precisely because of the enormous differences between the provinces and on the basis of the various investment and development programs in the area, in order to ascertain the effectiveness of a national law, it is necessary to consider its implementation at the provincial or local level.

So, a certain originality of the notion of the rule of law can be affirmed in the context of the PRC, not only in terms of the sources of legitimation of the rules, considering the morality of the political documents of the PCC, the economic efficiency that works as stabiliser of power, the transfer of the responsibilities of the PCC to the State Institutions (Ajiani), but also with reference to the bases of its legal system: its own traditions, the best foreign experiences, international provisions, international customs. The challenge that China was proposing in the first decade of the twenty-first century was the creation of high-quality legislation in favour of the people, that is, with a democratic orientation, and a scientific orientation, improving

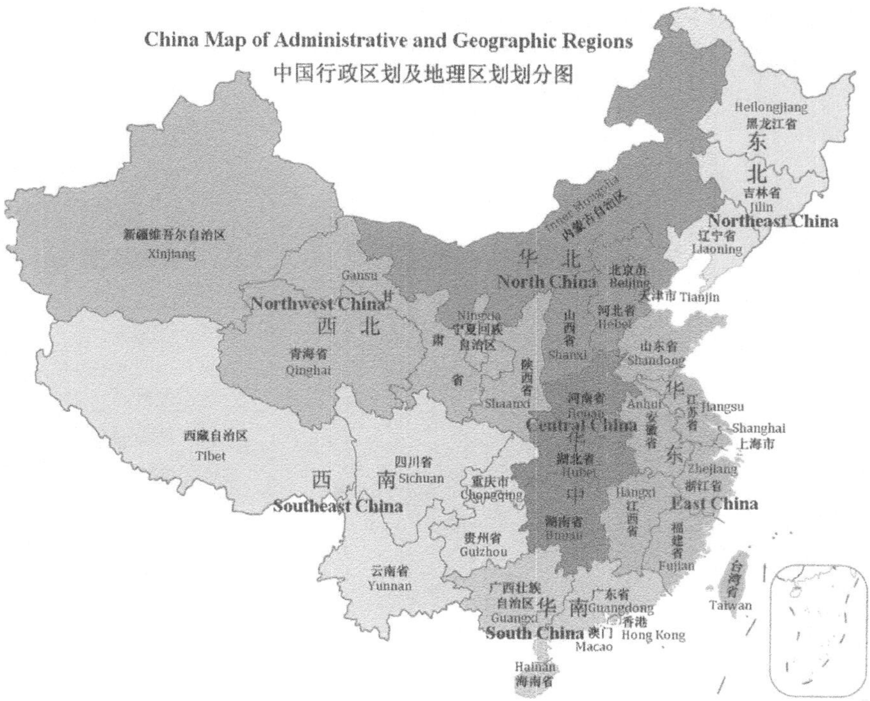

Fig. 3.1 *Source* https://www.chinadiscovery.com/china-maps/china-provincial-map.html

legislative technique: the objective of the Law it is the eradication of poverty, guaranteeing human rights, towards subsistence and development (land, property, quality of life). The legislation represents the organic unity of the PCC leadership, the concrete institutionalisation of the PCC's principles and policies, capable of systematising coherence between the PCC, the population, and the legal order (Li). We can decree this phase as finished, considering that with "Xi Jinping's thoughts on the rule of law" if he officially entered a "new legal era".

3.2 Constitutional Reforms

The textual amendments to the Constitution have surely represented the most visible change in the entry of new legal concepts into the PRC and the need to "internalise" them.

The 1982 Constitution, still in force, was inspired by some principles inserted by Deng Xiaoping: who proposed taking into account the reality of China and including the best of foreign experiences and ideas; limit itself to the norms that were essential for national unity, social stability and the four modernizations; be guided by four basic

Fig. 3.2 *Source* Caixin

principles (Preamble) of socialism (political modernization), dictatorship of popular-democratic thought (Democratic popular dictatorship and no more dictatorship of the proletariat), Marxism-Leninism, Mao Zedong.

The main objective of the constituents was to concentrate all efforts towards the modernization of Chinese socialism, both from the point of view of politics and the economic system. Next, the socialist State was given the task of leading the national economy to an important development of its structures, in such a way that the social needs of the people are guaranteed.

The 1988 reform was caused by the strong growth of China's economy within the framework of the international market and inspired two innovations: the legitimacy of the private economy and the possibility of transferring private use of public land.

The 1993 reform wanted to provide a stabilisation of the market economy and the progressive abolition of state economic planning.

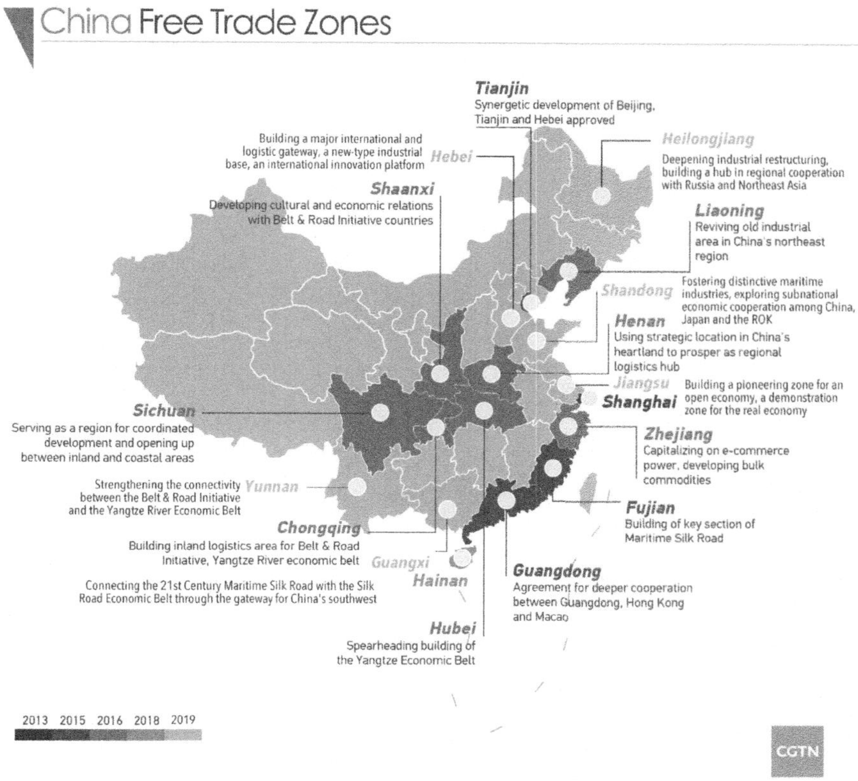

Fig. 3.3 *Source* GCTN

The 1999 reform was one of the most important because the principle of the "Rule of Law" was explicitly introduced, as well as the recognition of the value of the individual economy, which is defined as an "important constitutive aspect of the socialist market economy". The Article 5 of the current Constitution of the PRC states: "The People's Republic of China governs the country in accordance with Law and builds a socialist country governed by Law." This article was introduced with the 1999 reform, which proclaimed the principle of legality with the first paragraph (The PRC governs the country according to the Law) and what is defined as the Rule of Law ("with the intention of building a socialist State governed by law").

With the already mentioned 2004 reform, two innovations were introduced that reflect the need for the PRC to be in line with the basic principles accepted by other countries to promote dialogues—not only trade—with foreign nations. Article 13, which establishes that "private property is inviolable", and provides compensation in the event of expropriation or requisition of the land by the State; Article 33, which proclaims that "The State protects and guarantees human rights". This new formulation is characterised by the absence of reservations and this is undoubtedly a sharp change in direction compared to the past. Some researchers have claimed

Fig. 3.4 *Source* Asia Briefing Ltd

Table 3.1 *Source* Belt and Road Advisory

Overview of China's Special Economic Zone Classifications

Type	Full Name	Representative Examples	Start	Focus
SEZ	Special Economic Zone	Shenzhen, Zhuhai, Xiamen, Suzhou	1979	FDI, Factories, Outsourcing
ETDZ	Economic & Technical Development Zone	Pearl, Yangtze, Min River Deltas	1984	Industrial Parks, Assembly, Finishing
HIDZ	High-Tech Industrial Development Zone	ZhongGuanCun, Nanjing, Tianjin	1988	Technology Transfer, R&D, Trade
FTZ	Free Trade Zone	Shanghai, Tianjin, Hainan	1990	Streamlined Shipping, Trade, FOREX
EPZ	Export Processing Zones	Kunshan, Jinqiao, Wenzhou	2000	Export Processing, Bonded Warehouses
FTP	Free Trade Port	Hainan	2020	HK, SP style International Trade & Finance Hub

BELT & ROAD ADVISORY

For more information see: http://www.beltandroadadvisory.com

that it may mark the transition from an "Asian" or "Chinese" conception of human rights to a more "universal" view of the issue. Others have argued that this norm could be interpreted as a true "open norm", capable of extending the guarantees for rights not mentioned in the Constitution, and in particular the rights enshrined and guaranteed in international conventions that China has formally ratified. The new text of Article 33 has, in fact, assumed a fundamental role in a context of profound changes in Chinese society, which has led to an international vocation of its own scale of values and principles.[3]

Finally, the last reform of the Constitution is the one carried out in 2018. On this occasion, among the various amendments, there are three changes that are of interest for the purposes of this investigation: (a) Added to the Preamble the expression that China "will adhere to the path of peaceful development and the strategy of opening up of mutual benefit"; (b) greater legislative power has been attributed to a large number of cities, which will be able to sanction local laws and regulations directly, respecting the Constitution, provincial laws and regulations; (c) "Xi Jinping's thought on socialism with Chinese characteristics for the new era" and "the scientific conception of development" are incorporated into the Constitution.

(a) Under the first profile, the connection between China's national constitution and its international vocation is strong. The Chinese Constitution, as the highest source of law in the domestic legal system, constitutes at the same time the programmatic guideline document for the realisation of its own purposes not only in its own development but also in the dialogue relationship with the international community. All the modernity of the Chinese legal system converges in this modification: not only an internal discipline but also a global development.
(b) The second change is substantial, adding a further element to the "quality legislation" as it manifests the consolidation of the principle of non-contradiction between legal sources, and the derivation of the principle of hierarchy of sources. The lack of this "legal certainty" for many years has made the activity of legal and judicial operators very difficult, as it was often not clear which of the legal sources should prevail over the other, with a great variability of the legal discipline on one same sector depending on the province.
(c) The inclusion of "Xi Jinping's Thought on Socialism with Chinese Characteristics for the New Era" fuels the theoretical discourse already present in the Constitution. In particular, Xi's thought includes 14 points each, among which stand out various references to the importance of "governing the country through the law considered the basis of Chinese democracy" (point 5), "the centrality of the people with respect to the actions of the government " (point 2) and "the integral government of the country according to the law" as an "essential requirement and important guarantee of socialism with Chinese characteristics", with the aim of "building a single whole between state, government and society governed by law" considering the law as a fusion between "law and morality" (point 6). Furthermore, the constant reference to a "new concept of

[3] See Chap. 2.

development" in line with "scientific innovation and ecology" (point 4) is essential, capable of functioning as an "improvement of the living conditions of the population" through "equity, justice and liberation from poverty" (point 8), and capable of generating a "harmonious coexistence with nature" (point 9). Finally, the "construction with a community with shared future for mankind" is foreseen as an externalisation to the international community of the "Chinese dream", capable of creating a "peaceful international environment and a stable international order", considering "as a joint vision the national and international situation" (point 13).

Already in the last constitutional reform, this global yearning towards the construction of a community with a shared future for all peoples, who aspire to a development united by the dignity and full fulfilment of the human person, appears in a nutshell. The integration between the outside and the inside as an essential basis for a peaceful coexistence, as highlighted in the White Paper "China and the World in the New Era",[4] in which it is stated: "a path of development adapted to its real conditions and that constitutes an opportunity for the world towards the construction of a prosperous and beautiful world that is the common aspiration of all peoples".

3.3 Chinese New Civil Code: Unification and Humanism in Chinese Law

The Chinese legal experience sometimes is fragmented (Staiano, 2016), flexible (Castellucci, 2007) but several elements lead us to identify a conspicuous unification of the Chinese legal model, through: (a) the construction of a socialist rule of law with Chinese characteristics (Staiano, 2016); (b) a qualitative evolution of Chinese law, in line with the principles of international law (Staiano, 2014; Li, 2008; Liu, 2010); (c) the adoption of a Civil Code (Esborraz, 2019). The mix between the creation of modern legal science and the evolution of the Chinese moral sense is clear, and they cannot do without their cultural roots. The Chinese humanist turn, therefore, is not a novelty, but a modernization of legal culture. The civil code is one more confirmation of this. As stated by Xu Diyu: "The regulatory complex (of the civil code) makes great efforts to bring Chinese civil law into line with the rules commonly practiced internationally. At the same time, the typical substrate of the socialist economic system, the judiciary and the tradition of Chinese legal culture are also maintained" (Xu, 2021).

The adoption of the new Chinese civil code reveals a gap between the real and the symbolic. Western codes, in Europe in particular, are always thought of as the best legal experiences for several reasons. For its historical ties to Roman and medieval law; for its modernity and constant updating. On the other hand, as has been analyzed

[4] PRC State Council, *White Paper on China and the World in the New Era*, September 2019, available at https://english.www.gov.cn/archive/whitepaper/201909/27/content_WS5d8d80f9c6d0bcf8c4c142ef.html.

by Esborraz, the first civil code of the PRC, and the Argentine civil code as reformed in 2015, represent the only true codifications of the twenty-first century, including a series of legal institutes almost absent in European codes (Esborraz, 2019). Many are the analogous aspects between the Chinese and the Argentine code, especially with reference to the humanistic elements. As Esborraz emphasises with his deep research:

> From the comparison of both codifications, the community of concepts, principles, institutions and provisions existing between them emerges, which is justified by the fact that both orders belong to the Romanistic legal system. This can be seen, in particular, in the general system adopted by both Codes, as well as in the particular attention paid to the protection of the human or natural person and the environment. Belonging to the Romanistic legal system facilitates dialogue not only between the Argentine and Chinese legal systems, but also between the latter and the other legal systems that make up the Latin American Subsystem, since they are all based on the common tradition of Roman Law. In addition, all of this acquires particular interest in view of the relations that China is establishing with Latin America.
>
> (Esborraz, 2019: 335)

Regarding the "humanist" vocation of the Chinese civil code,[5] at least two aspects can be considered relevant for the purpose of this discussion: the "people-centred approach" and the "green principle". As stated by Wang Chen, Vice Chairman of the Standing Committee of the National People's Congress, in his report to the Third Session of the Thirteenth National People's Congress on May 22, 2020: "Codification of the civil code is an unavoidable requirement to improve the welfare of the people and safeguarding the fundamental interests of the greatest number of people".[6]

With reference to the human person, there are at least two cardinal signs: (a) Article 2 of the Law on the general part of civil law of 2017 that provides "civil law regulates personal relationships and property relationships between natural persons, legal persons, entities and organisations without legal personality situated on an equal footing"; (b) Book IV of the code entirely dedicated to personality rights (人格权编).

In the first chapter on General rules, the Article 990 provides a definition of Personality rights, as "the rights enjoyed by persons of the civil law, such as the right to life, the right to corporeal integrity, the right to health, the right to name, the right to trade name, the right to likeness, the right to reputation, the right to honour, the right to privacy, and the like". However, the second paragraph opens up precisely that "residual category" typical of open abstract cases, especially in terms of fundamental rights. Indeed, it provides that "In addition to the personality rights provided in the preceding paragraph, a natural person enjoys other personality rights and interests arising from personal liberty and human dignity".

Book IV on personality rights is divided into six chapters: General Rules (I), Rights to Life, Rights to Corporeal Integrity and Rights to Health (II), Rights to Name and Rights to Entity Name (III), Rights to Likeness (IV), Rights to Reputation

---

[5] The humanistic character of the new Chinese code is also supported by Esborraz (2019), p. 372, and other authors, as well as cited by Esborraz in note 144.

[6] Available at: http://www.mod.gov.cn/topnews/2020-05/22/content_4865574.htm.

and Rights to Honor (V), Rights to Privacy and Protection of Personal Information (VI). Furthermore, in the other books of the code there is room for the protection of personal rights deriving from other juridical situations, such as marriage. In these cases, in addition to the protection offered by the Code and other laws, if there is a legal vulnerability, reference will be made to the general part of the code (Article 1001).

This double opening of Book IV, in the initial open norm (Article 990) and in the final norm of the chapter on General Norms (Article 1001), outlines that precisely that open human rights protection system has been created, in line with Article 33 of the Constitution.

This aspect coincides with the strong development of the people-centered approach promoted by Chinese socialist policy. In this sense, we recall "Xi Jinping's Thought on socialism with Chinese characteristics for the new era", inserted in Chinese Constitution in March 2018, where "People-centrism" is a key aspect of all legal and economic instruments implemented by Chinese government; the construction of the socialist rule of law with Chinese characteristics, the moderately prosperous economy and the new normality. Personality rights are inserted in a special section of the civil code, not only representing an innovation at the level of civil law systematization, but also reflecting an evolution, in a civil key, as an operational corollary of the constitutionalization of fundamental human rights. Human rights, in fact, were already present in the Chinese Constitution, in Article 33, reformed in 2004, with a very general and open notion. However, the general theory of human rights law "with Chinese characteristics" has been merged with domestic law, providing a full title of implementation of these in the new code. At the same time, the right to dignity (人格 权 保护) had already been affirmed, at the opening session of the XIX National Congress of the Communist Party of China on October 18, 2017, as reported by the Supreme People's Court: "The right to dignity is a fundamental human right. Entering a new era, China's main social contradiction has changed, and now people's material demands have been basically satisfied, people's demand for dignity is stronger than before".[7] In fact, Article 109 of the General provisions of the civil code establishes: "The law protects personal liberty and the dignity of the natural person", endorsing the declaration of the Supreme Court and making it manifest.

The other element in line with Chinese humanism in which we can detect the peculiar encounter between man and nature, through the confluence of Confucianism and Taoism, is precisely the protection of the environment. Article 9 of the General Part of the Chinese Civil Code establishes: "in carrying out activities of a civil nature, subjects must contribute to the conservation of natural resources and the protection of the environment". The so-called "green principle" (绿色 原则), like personality rights, represents the result of a long process of legal evolution, in line with the objectives established by the CCP for the construction of an "ecological civilization"[8] and with the Chinese Constitution that establishes in Article 9: "[...]

[7] Available at http://english.court.gov.cn/2017-11/08/content_34308303.htm.

[8] This aspect is also marked by Esborraz. For a legal historical overview of the evolution of environmental law in China, see Esborraz, 2019, p. 387 (and references in notes 194 and 195); Toti E.,

The state ensures the rational use of natural resources and protects rare animals and plants. The appropriation or damage of natural resources by any organization or individual by any means is prohibited", and in Article 26: "The state protects and improves the environment in which people live and the ecological environment. It prevents and controls the risks of contamination and other audiences. The state organizes and promotes reforestation and forest protection".[9]

Domestic legislation on environmental protection has been conspicuous in China, as the international effort to reduce polluting emissions in order to achieve a "sustainable development." As stated by the Supreme People's Court, there are two fundamental principles that have allowed a mandatory application of environmental protection:

(a) The ecological and environmental damage compensation system (生态 环境 损害 赔偿 制度)[10] to which the Civil Code dedicates Chapter 7 of the Book 7 from Article 1229 to 1235: according to the system, the people or companies that cause environmental damage should not only assume administrative and criminal responsibility, but will also be responsible for repairing the damage they cause to the environment and pay compensation for any ecological or environmental loss they cause. The compensation will be collected by local governments as a kind of non-tax revenue. This pilot program was launched by the central government in some provinces in 2015 and has been extended to the entire country since January 1, 2018.

(b) The environmental protection tax (环保 税),[11] provided for by the Environmental Protection Tax Law, was approved at the meeting of the Standing Committee of the National People's Congress on December 25, 2016 and has been in force since January 1st 2018. It is the first law in China that imposes the collection of an ecological tax and aims to end the policies applied by some local governments that exempt companies that are large contributors to the local economy. Also force companies to update their technology and switch to cleaner production.

The "green principle" was added to the general part of the civil code, reserved for "fundamental rights", which marks its aspiration to the universal application of the entire population, natural or legal persons, assigning specific protection, in line with the evolution of international environmental law.[12]

Il diritto dell'ambiente della Repubblica Popolare Cinese, in *Leggi tradotte della Repubblica Popolare Cinese*, vol. VIII (*Legge sulla tutela dell'ambiente*), Torino, 2016, IX-XLIII; Xu Guodong, *Il diritto romano come ponte tra diritto cinese e diritto latinoamericano*, in Formichella L. – Terracina G. – Toti E. (coordinators) *Diritto cinese e sistema giuridico romanistico. Contributi*, Giappichelli, Torino, 2005, pp. 119–127.

[9] Text available at: http://www.leggicinesi.it/view_doc.asp?docID=384.

[10] Available at: http://english.court.gov.cn/2017-12/20/content_36013880.htm.

[11] Available at: http://english.court.gov.cn/2017-12/14/content_36013836.htm.

[12] Consider the United Nations International Conferences on the Human Environment in Stockholm (1972), on Sustainable Development in Rio de Janeiro (1992), Johannesburg (2002), the Millennium

What emerges from this brief analysis is the strong humanistic element, interpreted in the light of traditional Chinese thought and the modern definition of "human development", which includes sustainable development.[13] This content, which has permeated the "spirit of the laws" in the last forty years of normative evolution in China, today finds its most complete manifestation in the drafting of the new civil code, which functions at the same time as a moral and legal reference for all the citizens.

Chinese civil code has also had substantial social relevance for its sense of community. The spirit of community in the civil code, inspired at the same time by its own cultural experience and by the legal tradition of Roman law (Esborraz, 2019), is the internal manifestation of a broader community vocation.

References

Castellucci, I. (2007). *Rule of law with Chinese characteristics. Annual Survey of International and Comparative Law, 13*, 35–92.

Castellucci, I. (2012). *Rule of law and legal complexity in the People's Republic of China.* Trento.

Esborraz, D. F. (2019). Los nuevos Códigos civiles de la República Argentina y de la República Popular China confrontados: dos ordenamientos y un único sistema. *Roma e America. Diritto romano comune, Rivista di diritto dell'integrazione e unificazione del diritto in Eurasia e in America Latina, 40*, 335–390.

Granet, M. (1988). *La Pensée chinoise.* París: Albin Michel.

Habermas, J. (2016). *Legitimation Crisis.* Feltrinelli-IBS.

Jihong, M. (2008). "El Derecho Constitucional en China". In *Oropeza García Arturo, México-China; Culturas y Sistemas Jurídicos Comparados, Instituto de Investigaciones Jurídicas de la UNAM, México.*

Li, L. (2008). *Historia del Derecho Chino y su Sistema Jurídico Contemporáneo.* China Academy of Social Sciences Press.

Liu, H. (2010). *Los Derechos Humanos en China en el marco del Derecho Internacional.* China Academy of Social Sciences Press.

Severino, E. (2010). *Téchne: Le radici della violenza.* Rizzoli.

Staiano, M. F. (2014). *El ordenamiento jurídico de la República Popular China en el marco del Derecho Internacional: planificación familiar, migraciones y cooperación.* Instituto de Relaciones Internacionales, UNLP.

Staiano, M. F. (2016). *Las recientes evoluciones de las relaciones entre China y Latinoamérica: el caso Argentina.* Mercosur abc.

Weber, M. (1991). *L'etica protestante e lo spirito del capitalismo.* BUR Biblioteca Universale Rizzoli.

Xu, D. (2021). "Il modello cinese di codificazione cinese". In O. Diliberto, D. Dursi, & A. Masi (Eds.), *Codice civile della Repubblica Popolare Cinese.* Pacini Giuridica.

Development Goals (2000–2015) and the current Sustainable Development Goals of the 2030 Agenda and the United Nations Conferences on Climate Change (COP 21 and COP 25).

[13] To deepen these aspects, cfr. Cadìn R., *Profili ricostruttivi e linee evolutive del diritto internazionale dello sviluppo,* Giappichelli editore, Torino, 2019.

Chapter 4
Building a Community with a Shared Future for Mankind: Legal Internal Elements and International Vocations

4.1 The Idea of "Prosperous State" in China: Legal Humanistic Aspects

In China we can observe an innovative paradigm, towards the construction of a "Prosperous State", instead of a "minimal state"[1] (Staiano, 2021). As President Xi Jinping said, presenting his strategy towards the building of a "common prosperity" in China with the Taxation: "the stated objective of "common prosperity" is "to regulate excessively high incomes" in order to ensure "common prosperity for all".

[1] The dogma of the "Minimal State"has been nourished by the Western narrative over the last 40 years (Nozick, 1974; Wolff, 1991). The neoliberal development model, which has built the now generalized idea of the state as an enemy, as a limit to development and economic growth, has marginalized and strongly weakened the role of the state, making it now unable to face any emergency. This almost absolute and untouchable theoretical "trend" in the West has also been replicated at the regional level. The theory of the minimal State has also weakened the value of politics and policy-making: the depoliticization of problems has given rise to the illusion of state decisions as mere administrative applications, emptying their political contents. Consequently, there has been a progressive delegation of decisions to executive powers, Governments, with a simultaneous decrease in parliamentary activities, which was followed by a gradual lack of preparation of political representatives. The narrative of "youthful nihilism" (Galimberti, 2008) and the impossibility of "getting out of the post-democratic system" (Crouch, 2004), of an elusive "liquid society" (Bauman, 2007), served as an ideological basis to legitimize any decision taken in the name of the market. The population witnessing a progressive worsening of their living and working conditions, has begun to "abandon" political interest, having lost the importance of the national political debate, with a progressive erosion of the entire democratic system. The vulgarity and irrationality of the measures implemented by national governments (in absence of international cooperation) have provoked violent reactions, especially from workers who are subjected to macro-economic decisions every day in constant opposition to their fundamental rights. As UN Secretary General António Guterres pointed out in his speech during the 76th UN General Assembly on 21 September 2021, "the collapse of confidence is leading to a collapse of values" (Guterres, 2021). Staiano, M.F., *"Minimal State" & "Prosperous State": Technique or Humanity?*, in "Selected articles of the China-Argentina Economic Dialogue", September 2021, Chinese Academy of Social Sciences Press.

M. F. Staiano, *Chinese Law and Its International Projection*, Understanding China,
https://doi.org/10.1007/978-981-19-9578-1_4

The concept of "Prosperous State" has a very deep and long history: as described by Gallelli (2021) the expression 富强 (*Fùqiáng*) means "Prosperous and powerful". It crossed all Chinese political dimensions from Han Feizi to Xi Jinping trough Mao Zedong and Deng Xiaoping: in fact, there is a motto in China that says "with Mao the Chinese nation has risen to its feet, with Deng it has become economically prosperous, with Xi it becomes prosperous and powerful". So we can understand that the building of a prosperous State constitutes a process: in fact, observing Chinese way to a "Prosperous State", we can include at list eight fundamental elements, which represent Chinese innovations in the construction of a "Prosperous State": Socialist Market Economy, New Normal, Dual Economy, "Socialist Economic Development in the 21st Century" (Jabbour & Gabriele, 2021), Socialist Rule of Law with Chinese Characteristics, China-oriented Globalization, Belt and Road Initiative, Community with a Shared Future for Mankind.

According to He Yiting, Director of the Chinese Comunist Party School, what is happening now is a transition "from a Big Country (大国, *Daguo*) to a Prosperous Country (强国, *Qiangguo*)". Prosperous State also means that China is not willing to suffer another humiliation, or to give in on all those aspects which it defines as "crucial interests" (核心利益, *Hexin liyi*), in an autonomist perspective.

The idea of creating a prosperous state is associated with the concept of development. It has recently been reaffirmed by Xi Jinping and also added to the Party Constitution as statements on: "gradually realising the goal of common prosperity for all; having an accurate understanding of the new stage of development; applying a new philosophy of innovative, coordinated, green, open, and shared development; accelerating efforts to foster a new pattern of development that is focused on the domestic economy and features positive interplay between domestic and international economic flows; pursuing high-quality development; giving full play to the role of talent as the primary resource; and ensuring higher-quality and more efficient, equitable, sustainable, and secure development of the economy".[2]

Development is a common topic for the countries of the global south, but often not declined in its multidimensionality especially in international dynamics, as it is characterised by a profound asymmetry in the state of development of the various countries. If we think of the Sustainable Development Goals of the 2030 Agenda, for example, we cannot fail to notice that some fundamental objectives such as the elimination of extreme poverty and the eradication of hunger concern two thirds of the world's population and characterise a state of necessity fueled "by the world developed" (Panikkar, 2015).

According to Panikkar, the very concept of development appears "spoiled" by a typically Western conception, which is unable to summarise the potential for alternative development. Panikkar believes that the notion of development is a Western construction that "shows the initial bias", as "the very archetypes underlying the idea of development imply a mechanistic anthropology that three-quarters of the

[2] 20th CPC National Congress concludes in Beijing, Xi Jinping presides over closing session and delivers important speech, October 23, 2022, Xinhua; available at: http://english.www.gov.cn/news/topnews/202210/23/content_WS63551debc6d0a757729e1950.html.

world's population would find inadequate". This archetype as an ideal of human life is "especially open to criticism in its political by-products" (Panikkar, 2015: 38).

China has always considered development as a crucial element for the construction of increasingly advanced guarantees to generate human development that guarantees the full realisation of individuals and a harmonious society. In particular, the "quality of development" is in a more prominent position and underscores high-quality development in various aspects, including economy, society, culture and ecology. In the XX Congress of the Communist Party much emphasis was placed on planning a "new development philosophy on all fronts, focused on promoting high-quality development, and worked to create a new pattern of development", capable of "building a moderately prosperous society in all respects". This is inextricably linked to "developing whole-process people's democracy, and advanced law-based governance across all fields of endeavour".[3]

In fact, on a juridical level we have seen how among the characteristics of the Chinese rule of law there is a pre-eminence of economic, social and cultural rights, on the basis of which civil and political rights were later built. This is also confirmed by the ratification of the United Nations Covenant on Economic, Social and Cultural Rights in 2001, while the only signing of the United Nations Covenant on Civil and Political Rights dates back to 1998 and has not yet been ratified. Development is therefore at the heart of the international agenda as an essential centre of imputation of all human rights, which in fact depend on a substantial exit from a structural condition of poverty and social exclusion. China has lifted about 800 million citizens out of extreme poverty at the end of 2020, despite the severe crisis due to the COVID-19 pandemic (Tables 4.1 and 4.2). However, still "imbalances and inadequacies in development remain a prominent problem" as well as "wide gaps in development and income distribution between urban and rural areas and between regions" (Xi, 2022). The link between development, prosperity and democracy,[4] as goals inextricably linked to an innovative and moderate development to eliminate the country's

[3] Xi Jinping, Report to the 20th National Congress of the Communist Party of China October 16, 2022, *Hold High the Great Banner of Socialism with Chinese Characteristics and Strive in Unity to Build a Modern Socialist Country in All Respects.*

[4] Recently, on December 4th 2021 a White Paper on "China: Democracy That Works" was published by the Chinese State Council (available at http://www.china-embassy.org/eng/zgyw/202112/t20211204_10462468.htm). In this White paper we can find some elements of Democracy with Chinese characteristics: 1. Democracy as a common value of humanity and an ideal that has always been cherished by the Communist Party of China and the Chinese people. For the past hundred years, the Party has led the people in the realisation of people's democracy in China. According to the text, today the Chinese people truly take their own future and that of society and the country in their hands. 2. The status of the people as the owner of the country is the essence of popular democracy. In China, full-process people's democracy integrates process-oriented democracy with results-oriented democracy, procedural democracy with substantive democracy, direct democracy with indirect democracy, and popular democracy with the will of the state. It is a model of socialist democracy that encompasses all aspects of the democratic process and all sectors of society. 3. Democracy as a concrete phenomenon that is constantly evolving. Rooted in history, culture and tradition, it takes a diversity of forms and develops along the paths chosen by different peoples based on their exploration and innovation. The document indicates that democracy is a right of the peoples of all countries and not a prerogative of a few countries. Almost in these three elements we can find the essential

Table 4.1 *Source White Paper on China and the World in a New Era*, September 2019

Improvement of the Chinese people's living standards			
Year index	Early years after the founding of PRC	1980	2018
Proportion of rural population living under the current poverty line	Extreme poverty	96.2%	1.7%
Per capita disposable income	RMB98 (in 1956)	RMB171 (in 1978)	RMB28,228
Life expectancy	35	65	77
Infant mortality rate	200‰	48‰	6.1‰
Preschool enrollment rate	20%	95.5% (in 1978)	Completion rate of nine-year compulsory education: 94.2%
Average years of schooling for people aged 15 and above	80% illiterate	5.3	9.6
Gross enrollment rate for higher education	0.22%	2.22%	48.1%

structural inequalities, is well expressed by the construction of a moderately prosperous society, in the White Paper China's Epic Journey from Poverty to Prosperity.[5] In fact, this White Paper points out how *Xiaokang*, meaning moderate prosperity, has been a consistent aspiration of the Chinese nation since ancient times, and how this represents an alternative form of long-term development, which has evolved through the process with all dimensions of the problem of poverty.[6]

---

vocation to community and humanism in China, which confirm the "people-centred-approach" and the opening to new proposals to understand the long process of democratisation.

[5] PRC State Council, *White Paper on China's Epic Journey from Poverty to Prosperity,* September 2021, available at http://english.www.gov.cn/archive/whitepaper/202109/28/content_WS61528550c6d0df57f98e0ffa.html.

[6] There are almost twelve definitions of the term poverty (Spicker, 2009). As Spicker identified, these are generally divided into three main currents: material, economic and social conditions. Under the material concept, poverty is a lack of material goods or services, it is a core of basic needs and a set of other needs that change in time and space (George, 1988, p. 208); poverty is a severe deprivation of physical and mental well-being that is not connected with economic resources and consumption (Baratz & Grigsby, 1971, p. 120). Other researchers indicate that poverty is the lack of a certain kind of specific need; poverty refers not only to deprivation but also to deprivation suffered over a period of time (Spicker, 1993). From the economic perspective, poverty is related to the standard of living, that is, living with less than others. The International Labor Organization (ILO) considers that "at the most basic level, individuals and families are considered poor when their standard of living, measured in terms of income or consumption, is below a specific standard" (ILO, 1995, p. 6). Subsequently, the situation of inequality was also considered as poverty: people can be considered poor because they are in a disadvantaged situation compared to others in society (Miliband, 1974, pp. 184–185). According to the social concept, poverty is related to the absence of entitlements, lack of basic security, exclusion, dependency and social class.

Table 4.2 *Source* PRC State Council, *White Paper on China's Epic Journey from Poverty to Prosperity*, September 2021

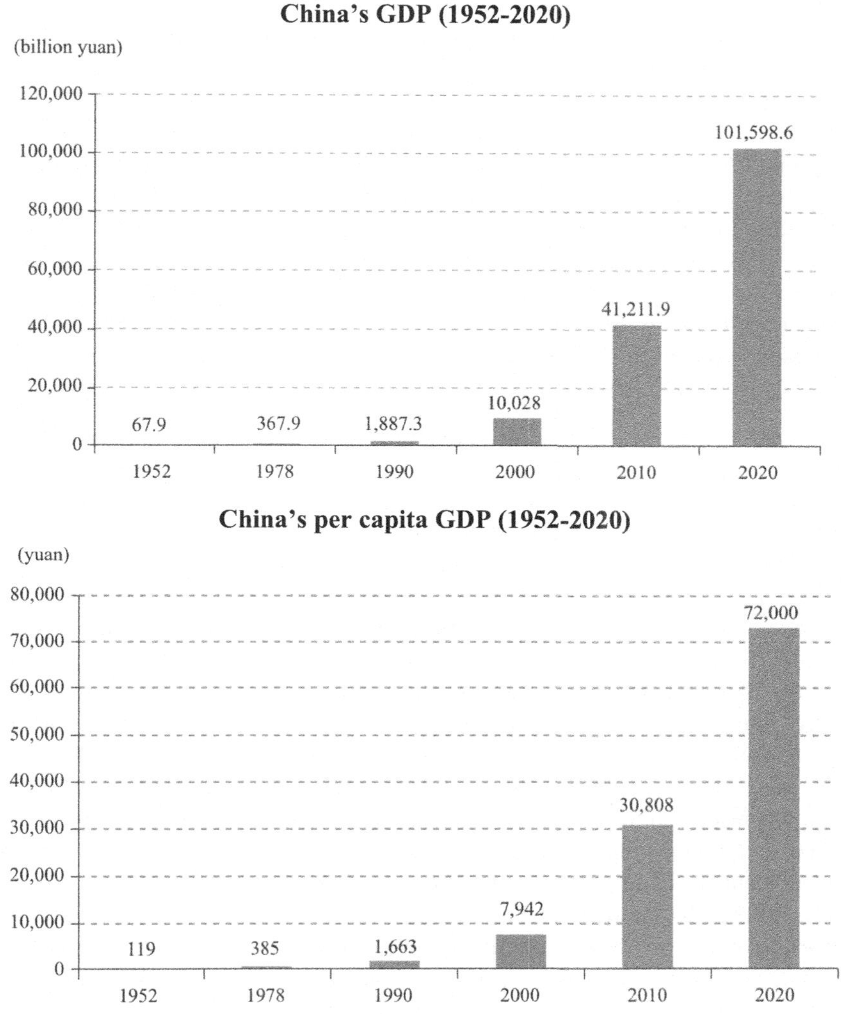

Box 4.1 China's Achievements in Poverty Elimination

Since the 18th CPC National Congress in 2012, China has launched targeted poverty alleviation and made notable progress. China's rural impoverished population was reduced from 99 million in 2012 to 16.6 million in 2018, a total reduction of 82.4 million, down by 13 million every year on average. China's poverty incidence dropped from 10.2 to 1.7%, down by nearly 9%

points. In 2019, China planned to help at least another 10 million poor and about 330 poor counties out of poverty.

Over more than 40 years of reform and opening up since 1978, according to the World Bank's international poverty line of US$1.9 per person per day, more than 800 million Chinese population have shaken off poverty, accounting for more than 70% of the global figure over the same period. China has become the first developing country to realize the poverty reduction objective in the United Nations Millennium Development Goals. UN Secretary-General António Guterres praised China as the largest contributor to global poverty reduction. In 2018, the UN General Assembly adopted a resolution on eliminating rural poverty, which included the concept and practice of targeted poverty alleviation initiated by China. China has provided a wealth of experience for the global fight against poverty.

In 1980, the World Bank defined poverty from the perspective of deprivation; it extended the purely material lack to the social, spiritual and cultural levels. In 1990, the "Human Development Report" presented for the first time the concept of "human poverty", which indicated that human poverty was not only one of income, but that it was the essential capacity to lead an acceptable life (World Bank, 1990). This new concept of human poverty that includes the denial of choice puts general attention on human development and opens the prelude to research on "multidimensional poverty". Later, in the "1997 Human Development Report", another new concept was proposed: Human Poverty Index (HPI), which does not use income to measure poverty, but rather the most basic description and expression of poverty indicators, such as short life and premature death, lack of basic education and inaccessible resources. In 2010, the UN development program reiterated the connotation of human development after summarising the experiences of the previous stage, and updated the poverty measurement indicator, which is the MPI, with the three dimensions: health, education and standard of living; its focus is to identify the multidimensional deprivation suffered by families. Precisely because of this complexity of the "poverty" theme, the result of Chinese politics is linked to an integration between politics, economics and law, where the affirmation of the principle of legal effectiveness and government through law represents a point of unification of all variables involved. In this sense, it is extremely relevant to the internal process of legal unification under the new Chinese Civil Code, especially in its humanistic perspective.

4.2 Building a Community with a Shared Future for Mankind: The Thought of Xi Jinping on Rule of Law

The Prosperous State is the internal face of a global governance strategy, proposed in its international vocation with "community with a shared future for mankind".

The idea of creating a "community with a shared future" emerged in September 2011 in the White Paper on Peaceful Development,[7] later upheld in Wen Jiabao's speech during the XIV China-ASEAN Summit[8] and taken up by Hu Jintao in the opening speech of the XVIII National Congress of the Communist Party in 2012, in which the expression was improved with the formula "human community with a shared future", later perfected by Xi Jinping in his famous 2015 speech, on the occasion of the 70th anniversary of the United Nations, "building a community with a shared future for mankind",[9] which includes five contents: political association, security, economic development, cultural exchanges and the environment. This perspective was taken up in the speech at the United Nations in Geneva in January 2017[10] and the idea of the essential need to "build a community with a shared future" was confirmed in October of the same year in the Report of the XIX National Congress of the Communist Party[11] and inserted, through Xi Jinping's Thought on Socialism with Chinese Characteristics for a New Era, in the Chinese Constitution with the March 2018 reform.

The international importance of this community vocation for the future of humanity and the planet has been manifested in numerous international summits

---

[7] Full text of the Document of the State Council of the People's Republic of China, *China's Peaceful Development*, 2011, available at http://english.www.gov.cn/archive/white_paper/2014/09/09/content_281474986284646.htm, accessed on 07/17/2020.

[8] WEN, Jiabao, 14th summit between China and the Association of Southeast Asian Nations (ASEAN) (10 + 1), Bali, Indonesia, November 18, 2011, Statement, available at http://english.qstheory.cn/news/201111/t20111121_124891.htm, accessed on 07/20/2020.

[9] HU, Jintao, "Firmly advance on the path of socialism with Chinese peculiarities and fight for the consummation of the integral construction of a Moderately prosperous society ", in 18 National Congress of the Communist Party of China (CPC), November 8, 2012, Beijing, Full text of the report, available at http://cr.chineseembassy.org/esp/zt/t992906.htm, accessed on 07/20/2020.

[10] XI, Jinping, "Working Together to Forge a New Partnership of Win-Win Cooperation and Create a community with a Shared Future for Mankind" (speech at the UN General Assembly, New York, September 28, 2015), https://gadebate.un.org/sites/default/files/gastatements/70/70_ZH_en.pdf.

[11] XI, Jinping, "Work Together to Build a community with a Shared Future for Mankind" (speech at the UN Office, Geneva, January 18, 2017), http://www.xinhuanet.com/english/2017-01/19/c_135994707.htm.

and Chinese foreign policy documents.[12] However, one of the most recent and relevant occasions is the Resolution 43/21 of the Human Rights Council of June 22, 2020 called "Promoting mutually beneficial cooperation in the field of human rights", in which the importance of promote international relations based on mutual respect, equity, justice and mutually beneficial cooperation and build a community with a shared future for mankind in which all enjoy human rights.[13] It should be noted, then, as the internationalisation of the community through the formula of "community with a shared future" coincides with the progressive affirmation of international human rights law in China: Liu Huawen underlines "international laws offer a legal consensus of community, or better said, a common norm"(Liu, 2010: 7).

The idea of creating a "community with a shared future" has common roots with similar concepts: the aspiration for a new humanism, in line with the construction of sustainable development with the support of the 2030 Agenda, has recently manifested at the global level: many intellectuals[14] in recent years have published texts and analyses in the hope of a new model of scientific, technical, moral and rational development that focuses on the human being in his natural context. Among these, one of the most incisive is undoubtedly Edgar Morin, who was the first to deepen the notion of "community with planetary destiny" (Morin, 2001: 120) theorised by Otto Bauer with the term *Schicksalgemeinschaft* (Bauer, 1907), later adopted by Chinese government with the expression "a community with a shared future for mankind" (*Renlei mingyun gongtongti,* 人类 命运 共同体).

The need for a "new type" "democratisation" of international relations for a more just and equitable international order, including visions from a Global South. The deepest and most articulated is the idea of generating a "community with a shared future for mankind", formulated by China and involving all aspects of international

---

[12] See the "Document on China's Policy towards Latin America and the Caribbean" of 2016. Already in the Foreword, emphasis is placed on globalisation and multipolarity to achieve the difficult goals of "peace world and common development". Likewise, reference is made to the need to "build international relations of a new type", with the win-win principle as the core and "to forge a community with a shared future for mankind". In this process, the aim is to "take the China-LAC international cooperation association to a New Height". "All countries, large or small, strong or weak, rich or poor, are all equal members of the international community." Full text of the Document available at https://www.fmprc.gov.cn/esp/wjdt/wjzc/t1418256.shtml, accessed on 07/20/2020.

[13] Full text of Resolution 43/21 of the Human Rights Council of June 22, 2020 called "Promote mutually beneficial cooperation in the field of human rights", available at https://undocs.org/es/A/HRC/43/L. 31/Rev.1, accessed on 07/22/2020.

[14] Knowing not to be exhaustive, we can mention the following texts: Morin Edgar, *I sette saperi necessari all'educazione del futuro,* Raffaello Cortina Editore, Milano, 2001; Prenna Lino, *Un nuovo umanesimo europeo. Popoli, religioni, culture,* Il pozzo di Giacobbe Editore, 2020; Ciliberto Michele, *Il nuovo umanesimo,* Editore La Terza, 2017; Ferrarotti Franco, *Dalla società irretita al nuovo umanesimo,* Armando Editore, 2020; Torres Mauro, *Un nuevo humanismo,* Biblioteca Nueva, 2018; Ikeda Daisaku, *El nuevo humanismo,* Tezontle, 2013; Daodonnet Luc, *Pour un nouvel humanisme,* Editions L'Harmattan, 2016; Okwa-Ondo Abraham-Peter, *Nouvel humanisme et ontologie africaine,* L'Harmattan, 2015; Chomsky Noam, *Le nouvel humanisme militaire,* Page 2, 2000; Matesanz Eva Maria, *Tout savoir sur l'art du lien: le nouvel humanisme connecté,* Kawa Tout Savoir Sur, 2014.

relations in a multidimensional and global way. This purpose has also been marked in the XX Congress of the Communist Party of China, as well as exposed in the Report of President Xi Jinping, in particular in chapter 14, where the connection between the structuring of the community with a shared future and the promotion of world peace and development.

The term community, in Western languages, is intrinsic in various meanings, especially in the field of political philosophy (Hobbes, Rousseau, Kant, Heidegger, Bataille, Nietzsche, Freud, Bauer, Morin, among others) and is usually associated with to an idea of *Res publica*, as a public good, in common, reducing it to a "common property". Many intellectuals, therefore, have used this term to speak of something "own", in "common", leading the discourse towards an "identity of the state". However, thanks to a semantic deconstruction reading of the term carried out by Roberto Esposito (2006), we can reinterpret this term in light of its authentic etymological root, from the Latin *Communitas*. Esposito affirms that "the common is characterised by the non-proprietary, the other", "the *communitas* is the set of people gathered not by a property, but by a debt (*munus*)". The *munus*, in fact, was a "gift that had the duty to give as a benefit received", therefore, the community is a set of subjects who are united by a duty, *cum munus*, but who in reality are perfectly alien to each others, "given to alterity".

In Chinese "community" is translated as 共同体, where 共 means "to share", but also in Chinese we have the equivalent of "public" 公, and 贡 which means "tribute" or "offering", a concept very similar to *munus*. It is as if ancient thought preserved in itself this double origin of the sense of community, as "participation of a due gift", as "common responsibility" towards the very idea of humanity. The same 共 of 共同体 is used in another key term of Chinese international relations, the international relations theory of symbiosis, precisely 共生 (Gòngshēng), which precisely aims to promote an awareness of the "necessary interdependence" between nations, through "coexistence" and "common effort" as a necessary "tribute" to solve global problems for all peoples. In fact, at an internal stance symbiosis system "pursues the value orientation of harmonious coexistence between subjects" (Wang & Hu, 2016), and its natural extension in an international dimension is the "community with a shared future for mankind" (Staiano, 2020; Jin, 2014): the "community with a shared future" proposes a diplomacy inspired by the common interests of the international community, capable of generating a new multipolar order in protecting international fairness and justice (Xi, 2022). It is in this sense that we have already analysed this trend as a manifestation of a "new Chinese humanism" (Staiano, 2020). As stated by Professor Jin Yingzhong:

> The community with a shared future for mankind is a historical category. It is gradually created by various symbiotic relationships formed, expanded, extended, and strengthened during the historical development of human beings. It exists in the process of historical evolution. "You are in me", "Everything is prosperous, and everything is damaged." The contemporary sense of the community with a shared future is the product of historical development. The emergence of the contemporary community with a shared future for mankind makes the individual development of any country and any actor have to consider how to face the integrity of the international society and how to coexist with others.

(Jin, 2014)

The community with a shared future for mankind, as a general objective of the internationalisation of a Prosperous State, makes underline a "dual circulation in Law", as in the economy. In fact, the Central Working Conference on the Comprehensive Rule of Law, held in November 16 and 17, 2020, formally established "Xi Jinping's thoughts on the rule of law", in which "an important part of Xi Jinping's Thought on Socialism with Chinese Characteristics for a New Era is the fundamental follow-up and action guide for the comprehensive rule of law." (Liu, 2020). This vision of a "comprehensive rule of law" represents an osmotic interaction between international law and Chinese domestic law, generating a "feedback" of Chinese law towards international law. The idea of a "Comprehensive Rule of Law" functions as an "organic connection between the national rule of law and the international rule of law" (Liu, 2020).

This therefore generated a political-juridical concordance between the current implementation of the **rule of internal law** and the creation of a **rule of international law**, through China's foreign relations policy. This new paradigm aims to build a new type of international relations,[15] of a people-centred-approach global governance. For example, according to Liu Huawen, the five principles of peaceful coexistence are an innovative proposal from China to international law.

> The Five Principles of Peaceful Coexistence are norms of international law pioneered by China, a contribution of China to international law, and a highlight in the history of the development of international law. Adherence to the Five Principles of Peaceful Coexistence has been written in the vast majority of bilateral treaties on the establishment of diplomatic relations between China and other countries, and is reflected in such international documents as the Declaration on Principles of International Law adopted by the UN General Assembly in 1970, and the Charter of Economic Rights and Duties of States adopted by the UN General Assembly in 1974. It means that countries with different social systems, levels of development and economic power can, in accordance with the Five Principles of Peaceful Coexistence, be equal in legal status, achieve a balance of rights and obligations in mutual relations, respect each other and live together peacefully. It is a progress in modern international law and a progress in the history of the development of international relations.
> (Liu, 2020)

4.3 The Materializations of a Prosperous State and Community with a Shared Future

In the White Paper "China and the World in a New Era",[16] it is asserted that "a prosperous and beautiful world is the common aspiration of all peoples" (Chap. III). In

---

[15] See Chap. 5.

[16] PRC State Council, *White Paper on China and the World in a New Era*, September 2019, available at: https://english.www.gov.cn/archive/whitepaper/201909/27/content_WS5d8d80f9c6d0bcf8c4c142ef.html.

this sense we can say that the aspirations of a materialisation of the universalist vocation of the Prosperous State model, in its international declination of the Community with a Shared Future for Mankind, are several. The most relevant are the Belt and Road Initiative (BRI) and the Global development initiative (GDI).

The BRI is a global cooperation project started in 2013 after the very famous Xi Jinping speech in Kazakhstan which aims to an eurasian connectivity strategy planned to unite Asia, Europe and Africa by land and sea, The Silk Road Economic Belt and the 21st Century Maritime Silk Road. In 2017 President Xi Jinping announced the globalisation of the strategy, so the Latin American countries also joined the BRI as its "natural extension" after the participation of the Presidents of Argentina, Chile and senior officials of Brazil, Mexico and Peru in the BRI Forum celebrated in Beijing. It is a multidimensional project, which is characterised by three cooperation 三共 (*San gong*),[17] five connectivities 五通 (*Wu tong*)[18] and six economic corridors 六廊 (*Liu lang*).[19] The project includes several priorities: infrastructure connectivity, industry, resource development, economic and trade cooperation, financial cooperation, cultural exchanges, environmental protection and maritime cooperation. Actually 138 countries already signed the Memorandum of understanding of BRI (Fig. 4.1).

The White Paper "China and the World in a New Era" establishes that "The Belt and Road Initiative is a platform for building a global community with a shared future, acting as a "boat" and "bridge" to promote world peace and development".[20] The BRI is an initiative inspired by a strong multilateralism, a more equitable governance, a multidimensional perspective (health, green, digital, tourism, technology) and a more connectivity and union, representing under an international economy perspective "a direct challenge to neoliberal globalisation" (Vadell-Staiano, 2020). It deconstructs the traditional division of roles between stronger and weaker countries, giving a voice to the peoples of areas long ignored in building the norms of international law: Africa, Eurasia, Latin America. The BRI has played an important driving role in the regional integration processes in Europe by highlighting the "grey spaces", deliberately left in the shadows by the European Union. These spaces have been skillfully filled by Chinese diplomacy, which has therefore restored considerable importance to the countries of Eastern Europe.[21] In the same way, China is gradually reactivating an equilibrium in Latin America, intercepting the traditional role of the "backyard of the United States" and integrating new protagonist aspects of the Latin American region (Staiano-Bogado Bordazar, 2019). China had developed the BRI project with a deep aspiration for international win–win and south-south cooperation,

[17] 共商 (*gong shang*): co-coordinate; 共建 (*gong jian*): co-build; 共享 (*gong xiang*): co-sharing.

[18] Policy coordination, facility connectivity, free trade, financial integration and People-to-people connectivity.

[19] China-Mongolia-Russia Economic Corridor, New Eurasian Land Bridge, China-Central Asia-West, Asia Economic Corridor, China-Indochina Peninsula Economic Corridor, China-Pakistan Economic Corridor and Bangladesh-China-India-Myanmar Economic Corridor.

[20] PRC State Council, *White Paper on China and the World in a New Era*, September 2019, p. 43.

[21] For example, the "17 + 1" Summit between China and 12 EU countries and 5 non-EU Eastern European members. http://www.china-ceec.org/eng/.

through additional variations such as "the Health Silk Road", "the digital silk road", "the educational silk road". China proposes the BRI project as an externalisation of a "common prosperity", in line with a "peaceful development" and the construction of a "community with shared future for mankind". The BRI therefore proposes to integrate the Sustainable Development Goals (Agenda, 2030), constituting a comprehensive cooperation instrument capable of generating greater complementarity, more just and inclusive global governance and autonomous development of the countries that are part of them.

In the light of international law, the BRI has raised the need for a new international judge: the China International Commercial Court. The Court was established by the Supreme People's Court of China (SPC) to adjudicate international commercial cases. CICC's objective is to try international commercial cases fairly and timely in accordance with the law, protect the lawful rights and interests of the Chinese and foreign parties equally, and create a stable, fair, transparent, and convenient rule of law international business environment. The First International Commercial Court is situated in Shenzhen, Guangdong Province, and the Second International Commercial Court in Xi'an, Shaanxi Province. The Fourth Civil Division of SPC is responsible for coordinating and guiding the two international commercial courts.

The GDI was announced by Xi Jinping in a speech at the UN General Assembly in September 2021, but it was already in a nutshell in the White Paper of January 2021

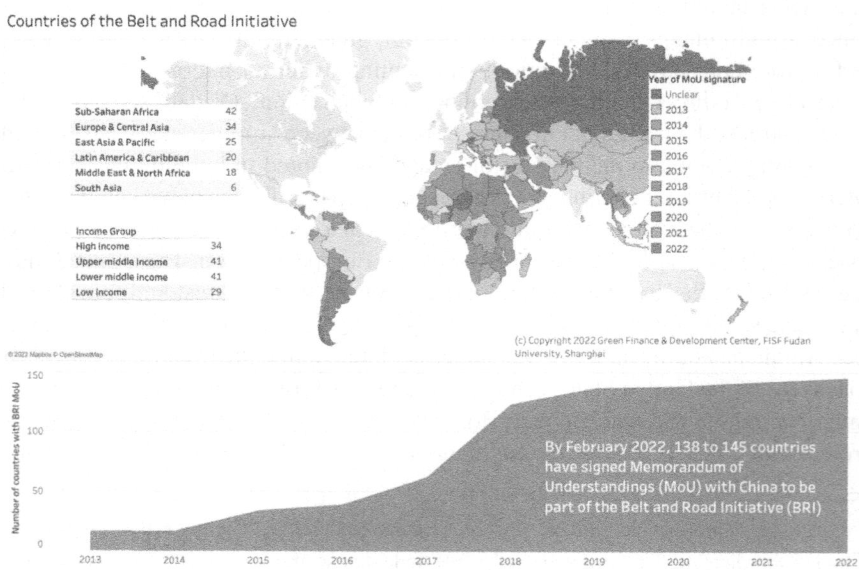

Fig. 4.1 *Source* https://greenfdc.org/countries-of-the-belt-and-road-initiative-bri/

"China's International Development Cooperation in the New Era",[22] which already established an aid plan for developing countries for the implementation of the 2030 Agenda as a key goal, in line with "global development partnership", an important part of the UN 2030 Agenda for Sustainable Development (Goal 17). The GDI is an "accelerator" of the United Nations Sustainable Development Goals and includes "six accompanying principles (a people-centred approach, development as a priority, benefits for all, innovation-driven development, harmony with nature, and action-oriented approaches), eight priorities (poverty reduction, food security, COVID-19 and vaccines, financing for development, climate change and green development, industrialisation, digital economy, and connectivity), governance arrangements, and actions" (Mulakala, 2022). It does not constitute an alternative to the BRI, but a parallel path to it, since "While the BRI is economic growth oriented, the GDI is development oriented. The BRI delivers hardware and economic corridors, while the GDI focuses on software, livelihoods, knowledge transfer and capacity building. The BRI is market oriented, where enterprises play a key role. By contrast, the GDI is public oriented, delivering grants and development assistance. While the BRI's pathways are mostly bilateral and regional, involving MOUs with partner countries, the GDI promotes diverse partnerships with multilaterals, NGOs and the private sector. China's National Development and Reform Commission is the main coordinating agency behind the BRI, whereas the Ministry of Foreign Affairs and the China International Development Cooperation Agency drive the GDI" (Mulakala, 2022).

The GDI plan, therefore, attributes a further framework of meaning to the construction of a Community with shared future, especially in relation to developing countries, through solid South-South cooperation also through the BRI.

4.4 Some Final Remarks

China is designing new internal and international schemes inspired by general principles shared by the international community and currently in existence: human rights, win-win cooperation, international solidarity, protection of natural resources, human development, among others. It seems that there is taking place in China that "double consciousness" barbarism-humanism described by Morin according to which "to the consciousness of barbarism must be integrated the consciousness that Europe produced—through humanism, universalism, the progressive constitution of a planetary consciousness—the antidotes to their own barbarism" (Morin, 2005: 109–110). China attributes a new framework of meaning to humanism through a new shared humanist mission, capable of aligning the Western democracies, which are now suffering a structural economic, social and cultural crisis, and the global South, which aspires to a rebirth to improve the life of their peoples.

[22] PRC State Council, *White Paper on China's International Development Cooperation in the New Era,* January 2021, available at https://english.www.gov.cn/archive/whitepaper/202101/10/content_WS5ffa6bbbc6d0f72576943922.html.

This ontological divergence between global issues and state actions constantly undermines state action, and represents an obstacle to overcoming a "egotic spirit" towards a "common spirit" of humanity. According to Teubner "the staggered nature of globalisation is the cause of an emerging hiatus between self-constituting autonomous global social systems, and their political legal constitutionalisation" (Teubner, 2010). And it can only be overcome through the construction of common actions, with international cooperation, based no longer on a "hostile" vision between states, but on a "communion" of intentions of the peoples, as new "global order and socio-economic relationships, pushing towards a breakthrough for a new world-system: not flat, not a pyramid but a real globe" (Herrmann, 2016).

"Prosperous State" as the new paradigm in a humanistic perspective, according to the Chinese New Humanism (Staiano, 2020): proposes the presence of a "strong and prosperous" state, a National responsibility with a People-centric approach, an International responsibility, in a Community with a Shared Future for Mankind, in which the Economy is subjected to a political control towards an affirmation of the Rule of International Law.

References

Baratz, M. S. & Grigsby, W.G. (1971). "Thoughts on poverty and its elimination". *Journal of Social Policy* (Cambridge), *1*, 2.

Bauer, O. (1907). *Die Nationalitätenfrage und die Sozialdemokratie*. Wien.

Bauman, Z. (2007). Liquid Times. Living in an Age of Uncertainty. Polity.

Crouch, C. (2004). *Post Democracy*. Polity.

Esposito, R. (2006). *Communitas. Origine e destino della comunità*. Torino: Einaudi.

Galimberti, U. (2008). *L'ospite inquietante. Il nichilismo e i giovani* The disturbing guest. Nihilism and young people, Feltrinelli.

Gallelli, B. (2021). *La Cina di oggi in otto parole*. Bologna: Mulino.

George, V. (1988). *Wealth, poverty and starvation*. Hemel Hempstead: Harvester Wheatsheaf.

Guterres, A. (2021). *Secretary-General's Address to the General Assembly*. Available at https://unric.org/it/discorso-del-segretario-generale-allassemblea-generale/

Herrmann, P. (2016). How Many Gigabyte has a Horse?; Seminar 'Continuidad y Cambios en las Relaciones Internacionales' at ISRI (Instituto Superior de Relaciones Internacionales Raúl Roas García), Habana.

ILO (1995). "The framework of ILO action against poverty" in Rodgers, G. (ed.) *The poverty agenda and the ILO*. Ginebra: International Labour Organization.

Jabbour, E., & Gabriele, A. (2021). *China. O socialismo do século XXI*. Brasil: Boitempo editorial.

Jin, Y. (2014). Shi lun renlei mingyun gongtongti yishi—jian lun guoji shehui gongsheng xing (On the consciousness of the community with a shared future for mankind—also on the symbiosis of the international society). *Guoji Guancha (International Watch), 1*, 37–51.

Liu, H. (2010). "Los Derechos Humanos en China, en el marco del Derecho Internacional". In *Revista del Instituto de Estudios Jurídicos de la Universidad Nacional Autónoma de México (UNAM)*.

Liu, H. (2020). "Lun Xi Jinping fazhi sixiang zhong de guoji fa yaoyi" ("On the essentials of international law in Xi Jinping's thought of rule of law"). *Bijiao Fa Yanjiu (Comparative Law Studies), 6*, 1–13.

Miliband, R. (1974). "Politics and poverty" in Wedderburn, D. (ed.) *Poverty, inequality and class structure*. Cambridge University Press.

Morin, E. (2001). *I sette saperi necessari all'educazione del futuro.* Milano: Raffaello Cortina Editore.

Morin, E. (2005). *Breve historia de la barbarie en Occidente.* Paidós: Buenos Aires.

Mulakala, A. (2022). *China's global development initiative: Soft power play or serious commitment?, October 18.* https://devpolicy.org/chinas-gdi-soft-power-play-or-serious-commitment-20221018/.

Nozick, R. (1974). *Anarchy, State, and Utopia.* Basic Books.

Panikkar, R. (2015). *Ecosofia. La saggezza della Terra.* Milano: Editoriale Jaca Book.

Spicker, P. (2009). Definiciones de pobreza: doce grupos de significado. *Pobreza: un glosario internacional.* CLACSO.

Staiano, M.F. & Bogado Bordazar L.L. (2019). "La iniciativa la Franja y la Ruta: innovación propulsora de los procesos de integración regional a nivel global. Los casos de Europa y América Latina". 一带一路倡议:将区域一体化升级至全球层面 的推动性创新。欧洲与拉美的案例. In Staiano, Maria Francesca - Bogado Bordazar, Laura L. - Caubet, Matías, *China: una nueva estrategia geopolítica global (la iniciativa la Franja y la Ruta)*, Universidad Nacional de La Plata Press, pp. 135–145.

Staiano, M.F. (2020). El neo-humanismo chino: un nuevo paradigma jurídico e internacional en las relaciones internacionales China-América Latina [Chinese neo-humanism: a new legal and international paradigm in China-Latin America international relations], *Brazilian Journal of Latin American Studies, Special Dossier on China – Latin American and Caribbean , 19*, 37.

Staiano, M.F. (2021). "Minimal State" & "Prosperous State": Technique or Humanity? *Selected articles of the China-Argentina Economic Dialogue*, Chinese Academy of Social Sciences Press.

Teubner, G. (2010). "Constitutionalising Polycontexturality". *Social and Legal Studies*, (vol. 19).

Vadell, J. & Staiano, F. (2020). "China en los intersticios de la crisis del multilateralismo y la globalización neoliberal: La Franja y la Ruta en Europa y el caso italiano". *Araucaria. Revista Iberoamericana de Filosofía, Política, Humanidades y Relaciones Internacionales, 22*, 45.

Wang, S., & Hu, S. (2016). Gongsheng zhexue lun (symbiosis philosophy outline). *Journal of Chang'an University (Social Science Edition), 18*(3), 71–84.

Wolff, J. (1991). *Robert Nozick: Property, Justice, and the Minimal State.* Cambridge Polity Press.

World Bank (1990). *World Development Report 1990: Poverty* (Washington DC).

Xi, J. (2022). Report to the 20th national congress of the communist party of China October 16, 2022. In *Hold high the great banner of socialism with Chinese characteristics and strive in unity to build a modern socialist country in all respects.* https://www.fmprc.gov.cn/eng/zxxx_662805/202210/t20221025_10791908.html.

Chapter 5
Building a Community with a Shared Future for Mankind in International Law Through the Chinese International Relations Theories

5.1 Chinese Characteristics and Their Importance

In 1982 at the XII Congress of the Communist Party, Deng Xiaoping proposed the definition of "socialism with Chinese characteristics". After the 19th CPC Congress in October 2017, in March 2018, Xi Jinping Thought on "Socialism with Chinese characteristics for a new era" was added to the Constitution. The application of the additional "with Chinese characteristic" to different fields represents a new strategy that affected all sectors of the People's Republic of China, generating a change in the country's internal and international policy. In economy, the proposals of "new normality", of "moderately prosperous society", "dual economy" were installed; in the legal sphere, a "socialist state of law with Chinese characteristics" has been created; in politics, we already mentioned "socialism with Chinese characteristics" and recently, in international relations, we find the "international relations theories with Chinese characteristics." As these theories develop, we are witnessing a gradual semantic and semiotic "shift" in the linguistic expressions of international relations.

Under a strictly methodological profile, some Chinese authors write about "International Relations Theories with Chinese characteristics", others prefer to speak of "Chinese schools of international relations", in a very articulated debate[1] that inquires several questions: what does "Chinese school of international relations" mean? Something that contains Chinese characteristics or styles? Something that has Chinese culture as its code? If a theory is Chinese, does it mean that it was

[1] The general debate about the compatibility of the theories of Chinese international relations or Chinese Schools of International Relations is very dense. For those who would like to know more, it is recommended to read the following monographs in English, not exhaustive of the subject in question: Arlene B. Tickner & David L. Blaney (2013), *Claiming the international*, Routledge, London and New York; Zhang Yongjin & Chang Teng Chi (2016), *Constructing a Chinese School of International Relations (Ongoing debates and sociological realities)*, Routledge, London and New York; Wang Hung-Jen (2013), *The Rise of China and the Chinese International Relations Scholarship*, Lexington Books, UK.

M. F. Staiano, *Chinese Law and Its International Projection*, Understanding China,
https://doi.org/10.1007/978-981-19-9578-1_5

created by Chinese researchers or in Chinese territory? Another question that arises is: can a Chinese theory have an universal value? Other authors indicate that the importance of the subject must be limited because in reality there would not yet be a "Chinese school", with Chinese international relations theories being an "objective and not yet an existing subject" (Ren, 2016: 46), or it would not be truly novel, representing the way to "be domesticated in another variable of Westphalianism", because "declaring a Chinese theory of international relations would negate its very attempt at originality" (Ling, 2016). In any case, the theorising of a Chinese school of international relations is "inevitable" (Ren, 2016: 44, 47), especially because of a "serious lack of theoretical innovation" in the matter (Ren, 2016: 43; Yu, 2005). However, it is true that we are witnessing a "decline of Western theories with a respective rise of non-Western theories" (Ren, 2016: 45).

All these academic discussions about the possible existence of a Chinese school of international relations constitute by themselves a relevant element because they highlight the need for new perspectives in the "Western-dominated" field of international relations. For example, Ren Xiao of the Fudan University of Shanghai has cogently argued for the need to detach international relations studies from the positivist scientific method, and has advocated for a return to a more cosmopolitan methodological pluralism, especially in the field of social sciences in which human actions are the object of research, and cannot be interpreted by the same methods as the "exact sciences" (Ren, 2016: 42). As Qin Yaqing noted, it is necessary to foster "a humanistic spirit integrated into the social sciences" (Qin, 2004). Likewise, L.H.M. "Lily" Ling deems how "the modernization (*westernisation*) of Confucianism has meant, in reality, the development of patriarchy, with the corresponding abandonment of the traditional patriarchy-matriarchy shared power" (Ling, 2016: 17–18), pointing out also the absence of a theorization in line with gender ideas, but inspired by a "muscularity" of international relations.

From these reflections, as well as from Qin Yaqing's comprehensive study of the stages of development of international relations theories in China, we can summarise two elements: that many of the theories developed by Chinese researchers are derivations and interpretations of Western schools: (a) not only in regard to their contents (realism, constructivism, liberalism, etc.), (b) but also as a method (scientific method). So what would be the novel elements in Chinese theories? First, recognizing these limits implies understanding the need for a change in method, as Ren Xiao has proposed; in the second instance, changing the research terms according to the linguistic mutation of the praxis of international relations, enriching the studies of this thematic area, could lead to a new theory of international relations. Under the first profile, Chinese research on international relations' multidimensionality and multidisciplinarity has extraordinary relevance. This factor is of utmost importance because international relations are interpreted under a rationalist paradigmatic model that has been proclaimed as such in the so-called mainstream (Simonoff & Briceño Ruiz, 2017: 45), and it is very difficult to subvert. In China, we are witnessing a "holistication" of the study of international relations through multidisciplinary approaches, with acknowledgments that goes through history, sociology, philosophy, biology, law, etc. In this sense, and coming to the second novel element of the Chinese theoretical experience, new contents are being developed in greater depth: harmony, *Tianxia*, peaceful development, Chinese dream, among others. In particular, four expressions help us to understand this process: (1) the "relational" theory of international relations; (2) human authority; (3) the symbiotic international system, and (4) community with a shared future for mankind.

5.2 The Main Chinese International Relations Theories

5.2.1 The "Relational" Theory of International Relations

The concept of "relationality" was theorised by Qin Yaqing, starting from the observation of the absence of a theory of relations and the need for a rational relations theory (Qin, 2011a: 250). Qin focuses his theory on the concept of relationships in their dynamic rather than static aspect, insisting on the concepts of meta-relationships and "relational-governance." The idea of meta-relationships merges with the Yin Yang dialectic that works as the "relationship of relationships", in the sense of the continuous effort to reach an agreement between opposite poles. Qin adjusts this element often associated with the Daoist tradition to the ontological divergence between norms and institutions that interact through a process of harmonisation and integration, attainable with the *Zhongyong*, the "golden mean" (Kumar, 2018). With reference to relational governance, Qin emphasises relationships as the only method capable of ensuring stability and order, as provided by Confucian philosophy, through morality and trust (Qin, 2011b: 133). According to Chinese culture, the essence of man is in the relationship and his capacity for relationality is an integral part of his sense of humanity. The term "benevolence" or "feeling of humanity" is expressed with the ideogram 仁 (*ren*) which is formed by the word 人 (*ren*) –with which it also shares the pronunciation– which means "person" and the number two (二), implying that the relationship with the other is constitutive of the human being, representing his spirit, his nature, his profound purpose.

A concrete example of the "cultural" obligation to undertake and maintain international relations with all states are not only the White Papers of the Chinese government on Chinese foreign policy (such as the two Documents of the Chinese foreign policy towards Latin America and the Caribbean of 2008 and 2016), but also the traditional Chinese practice that invents alternative forms of interinstitutional dialogue to bring together rational and relational interests (in this sense the "17 + 1" platform with Eastern European countries was pioneered) (Staiano & Vadell, 2020).

5.2.2 Human Authority

"Human authority" is an expression used by professor Yan Xuetong who has inaugurated the "School of International Relations" at Tsinghua University (Creutzfeldt, 2012), the so-called "Qinghua approach" (Kim, 2016: 72). His idea is that the theories of international relations are universal, so "Chinese characteristics" are not proposed as a distinctive element but as integrative contents to improve contemporary theories. In fact, international relations theories are totally dominated and shaped by the history and conceptual language of Western countries. So, the purpose of Yan is to add to this metalanguage the lexicon of the thinkers of ancient China (Yan, 2011: 8). It is the important concept of "human authority" of Xunzi (313–238 BC) that Yan emphasises. In Xunzi's political philosophy, a fundamental role was assigned to the hierarchy among states: the most powerful had an extra responsibility to maintain interstate order. This power is manifested in three different ways: tyranny, hegemony and human authority. Tyranny is based on military force and tactics, which can only lead to enemies and is therefore bound to lead to war. Hegemony, unlike tyrannical power, maintains a better level of morality in the sense of not betraying its State and its allies, but it is always based on a strictly dominating power. Human authority is the highest stage of power of a State, and is characterised by having a strong moral power of the rulers: the leader plays an active role in establishing interstate norms, generating changes in the system of relations with other states. Human authority, 王权 (*wangquan*), is made up of two words: 权 (*quan*) "authority", "power", and 王 (*wang*) which literally means "king", "emperor", "better or stronger than his peers". With the term authority is meant the fact of having strong material and political power, which gives it great responsibility. With the adjective "better or stronger than their peers", declined as "human", the need to have friends through relationships is pointed out, that is, more than allies, exercising friendly leadership over them (Creutzfeldt, 2012: 2). In fact, in the concept of human authority, political power and material power converge, in the sense that human authority always needs strong power, also supported by an efficient political system (Creutzfeldt, 2012: 2).

Clear examples of China's role as an "internationally recognized authority" are its actions in support of peace in international conflicts (such as in Ukraine), as well as Chinese health aid during the severe global COVID-19 pandemic (Staiano & Marcelli, 2020).

5.2.3 The Symbiotic International System

The symbiotic international system is a theory proposed by the so-called "Shanghai School", which has combined knowledge from sociology, biology and philosophy with international relations. The term 共生 (*Gongsheng*), symbiosis, has its etymology in the biological sciences, and the two parts of the word coincide with the Greek etymon of the word in English. In fact, 共 (*gong*) means "together" and

生 (*sheng*) means "live", "life", as well as in Greek σύν, "with, together" and βιόω, "live" (from βίος "life"). As in biology, where symbiosis indicates various forms of coexistence between organisms of different species, animals or plants, called "symbionts" and different modalities of symbiosis are defined according to the type of relationship that exists between them, in the same way the studies of the Shanghai school discard the idea that state and sub-state actors can exist independently of each other, defining antagonism as "you without me and I without you" (Su, 2016). This theory, therefore, foresees the need for each country to support and receive, in turn, the support of other countries in its development to guarantee its own stability (Mokry, 2018), generating in some way a "necessary interdependence" between nations. According to Hu Shoujun, the symbiotic system represents a positive vision about social evolution, an alternative to the Hobbesian or Darwinian one, and consists of three elements: (1) it is a totally endogenous process, in which all phenomenons generated in this system totally depend from individuals and their behaviours, therefore, every social system results as a local "closed system"; (2) all symbiotic relationships are complex, mutually conditioning each other; (3) the elements of the system are symbionts, therefore linked by a relationship of dependence for their existence.

Since the late 1990s, Hu Shoujun took a sociological approach in his analysis of Chinese society's processes of "democratisation", and began to develop his insights into the notion of symbiosis." However, this clash between individuals is bound to result in coexistence, because "the constraints of social symbiosis", including "law, morality, style and habits, religion, ideology, conventions" are often "intertwined" (Hu, 2006, 2012). Subsequently, Hu's symbiotic theory was proposed as a possible approach for international relations by Tang Shiping, Jin Yingzhong, Ren Xiao, in line with the progressive development of the international relations theories which were developing in China. Tang Shiping analyses the passage "From Biological Evolution to Social Evolution", proposing social evolution as a "phenomenon", through a very profound analysis in terms of genes, phenotypes, individual organisms and groups of individuals; and as a "dogmatic model" of development (Social Evolution Paradigm or SEP) and shape of the Social Evolution of International Politics, consequently for the evolution of the theories of international relations (Tang, 2013). The systemic order theorised by Tang places emphasis in the evolutionary process as well as in the meaning of a system that is externalised between the nation-states through relations, which manifest themselves with the need of cooperation and mutual respect, especially in relation to the own sovereignty and that of other states, through a peaceful coexistence between them.

The peaceful development, as an essential key-factor and as a consequence of a symbiotic international order, is a crucial element. According to Jin Yingzhong, who based his research largely on Hu's findings, the symbiotic "harmony culture" in China includes the symbiosis of individuals and the symbiosis of the country, and that human beings face a symbiotic society with connected destinies: all these factors of symbiosis are in Chinese traditional culture such as "community" and "harmony" (Jin, 2016). "'Symbiosis' is the basic way of existence of the international community. The symbiosis of the economic life of human society is a huge driving force that nurtures, forms and strengthens the international social symbiosis network. (…) One of its important features in peaceful developing age is that the situation of co-existing and interacting for international symbiotic system and the worldwide system in the international community's co-existing network, hence, at the meanwhile of priority to realise to develop and reform for the worldwide system co-existing relation it seeks to develop and innovate in the international symbiotic system co-existing relation" (Jin, 2011).

The Chinese theory of symbiosis is extremely articulated across the various disciplines it involves and harmonises: the search for not only an alternative but an evolutionary system of international relations appears strong, capable of "replacing the hegemonic international system" (Jin, 2014), with a new creative spirit. It represents "the concept that most reflects China's effort in terms of building the international order" (Su, 2016), because it is linked to the ideas of international cooperation in a Win-Win and South-South approaches, and also with China's leading role in building a new international order). Some examples of this can be the "neighbourhood policy" undertaken by China through infrastructure and global governance projects such as the Belt and Road Initiative, the recent Regional Comprehensive Economic Partnership agreement (RCEP), as well as the participation and promotion of various alternative and innovative international platforms, such as the Group of the "17 + 1" and the "BRICS". Through these practices, China has shown the will to generate long-term partnerships based not only on hard economic relations but also on changing and regenerative constraints of development and international cooperation models, seeking a symbiotic evolution of the international order.

5.2.4 The Community with a Shared Future for Mankind

The last expression to analyse is that of "a community with a shared future for mankind", 人类命运共同体 (*renlei mingyun gongtongti*), which is presented as a key objective of China's international relations towards the creation of a new international order. It has to be interpreted as including the three expressions already explained of "relationality", "human authority" and "symbiosis". The community with a shared future for mankind represents "a new global governance solution proposed by China", which provides for the creation of "a five-in-one global community" including "politics, security, economy, culture and ecology" (Li, 2017: 337). The "community" refers to the set of States, small and large, that peacefully coexist with each other (relationality) through common values inspired by the leading countries as those responsible for the international order (human authority), respecting and helping each other (symbiosis). In fact, the "community" does not refer "strictly to a right but to a responsibility" (Feng, 2017). The most difficult issue for the international community to understand is surely China's leading role as one of those responsible for international peace and security implicit in the expression "human authority". This element can be understood only by analysing the term *wang* in order to express some Chinese views on human authority, scholars have suggested the need to analyse the different applications of the concept *wang* in traditional political thought and its applications in contemporary international relations. There are authors who wrote on "Wangcracy" and "Wangrencracy", deepening the difference between the concept of 王道 (*Wangdao*), the king's way of governing, as opposed to 霸道 (*Badao*), the hegemon's way of governing (Tan, 2015).

5.3 Building a Community with a Shared Future for Mankind: From Theory to Practice

If we think of the expression "community with a Shared Future for Mankind" as an evocative container for the theories of international relations with Chinese characteristics, we must note its constant reference at the international level (Table 5.1), now consolidated not only in Chinese documents, but above all in the binding legal acts of the United Nations. The notion features at the core of China's foreign policy, and has been highlighted in many international resolutions in 2017. On February 10th, the concept was incorporated for the first time in a UN resolution, which called on the international community to enhance support for Africa's development "in the spirit of win–win cooperation and to create a shared future, based upon our common destiny." On March 17th, the notion of a "community with a shared future for mankind" was written in UN resolution 2344, related to promoting peace and stability in Afghanistan and the surrounding region. And on March 23rd, the UN Human Rights Council adopted two resolutions on the "Question of the realisation in all countries of economic, social and cultural rights", and the "Right to Food". Both the resolutions called for efforts "to build a community with a shared future for human beings", marking the first time that the concept has been recorded into UN Human Rights Council resolutions. The Committee of Disarmament and International Security of the 72nd Session of UN General Assembly, on November 6, 2017, approved two draft resolutions on the prevention of an arms race in outer space: "No first placement of weapons in outer space" and "Further practical measures for the prevention of an arms race in outer space."Both incorporated the concept of building a "community with a shared future for mankind." In the resolutions, the General Assembly encourages "all States, especially space-faring nations, to consider the possibility of upholding, as appropriate, a political commitment not to be the first to place weapons in outer space," and calls for agreement" on a balanced program of work that included the immediate commencement of negotiations on an international legally binding instrument on the prevention of an arms race in outer space." On June 22, 2020 the Human Rights Council's Resolution 43/21 entitled "Promoting mutually beneficial cooperation in the field of human rights", recognizes the importance of promote international relations based on mutual respect, equity, justice and mutually beneficial cooperation and "build a community with a shared future for human beings" in which all enjoy human rights.

Table 5.1 *Source* Personal elaboration

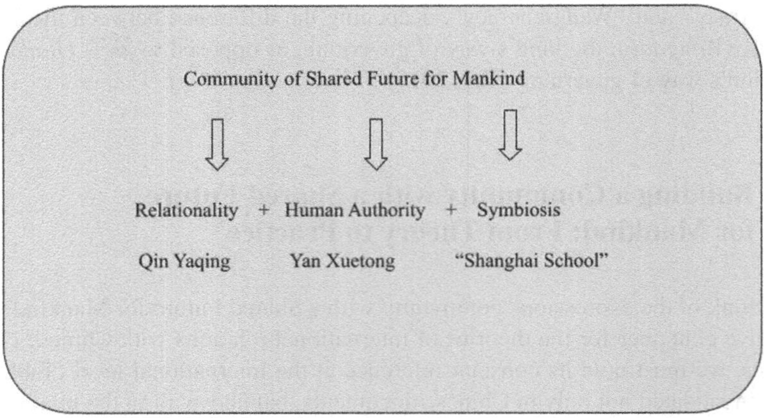

5.4 Some Final Remarks

In conclusion, Chinese Theories of International Relations present elements of innovation in the field of international relations, which in practice already have empirical results and mark the beginning of a new development, a "new era" of international relations at the global level. The Belt and Road Initiative, as the "materialisation" of the "community with a shared future for mankind", carries out the overcoming of realist theories as expressions of the mere national interest of each nation-state, enclosed in the post Westphalian concept of sovereignty, to interact internationally, and proposes a diplomacy inspired by the common interests of the international community, capable of generating win–win cooperation, towards a more just and equitable international order (Su, 2019: 12). In fact, only by combining these aspects under a comprehensive framework for international relations, as it was done from a juridical perspective with the thought of Xi Jinping on the Rule of Law (Liu, 2020),[2] we can understand the extent of a "responsibility for global symbiosis", with the effect of "communization" of global interests and fears, through a "process of human globalization" (Wang & Hu, 2016). In conclusion, in China the internal and international vision of a "people-centred-approach" in a global governance perspective through a "comprehensive rule of law" is fundamental to understand the new global order that is trying to merge human civilizations at a basic level of fundamental rights, building a community with a shared future for mankind.

The new era is a challenge towards a transition, towards new forms of relations and human development: what is at stake is not "simply" a new international order but a project of humanity that includes all visions and projections of social justice.

[2] See Chap. 4.

The world can no longer tolerate war as an instrument of international relations, nor submit to the nuclear threat. The "spirit of the peoples" is already much more evolved and in line with a "new planetary era" (Morin, 2001).

References

Creutzfeldt, B. (2012). "Theory talk #51: Yan Xuetong on Chinese realism, the Tsinghua school of international relations, and the impossibility of harmony". In *Theory Talks, November 28*.

Feng, W. (2017). "Common development, common values and the new international order". In *The collected works at the symposium on China studies*. Shanghai.

Hu, S. (2006). *Shehui gongsheng lun (A theory of social symbiosis)*. Shanghai: Fudan University Press.

Hu, S. (2012). "Guoji gongsheng lun (International symbiosis)". *Guji guancha (International observation). Shanghai International Studies University, 4*, 35–42.

Jin, Y. (2011). Guoji shehui de gongsheng lun: Heping fazhan shidai de guoji guanxi lilun (Symbiosis theory of international society, the theory of international relations of peaceful development era). *Shehui Kexue (Social Sciences), 10*, 12–21.

Jin, Y. (2014). Shi lun renlei mingyun gongtongti yishi—jian lun guoji shehui gongsheng xing (On the consciousness of the community with a shared future for mankind—also on the symbiosis of the international society). *Guoji Guancha (International Watch), 1*, 37–51.

Jin, Y. (2016). Shehui gongsheng yanjiu di dang dai xing (The contemporary nature of social symbiosis research). *Journal of Chang'an University (Social Science Edition), 18*(3), 71–84.

Kim, H. J. (2016). "Will IR theory with Chinese characteristics be a powerful alternative?" *The Chinese Journal of International Politics, 9*, 59–79.

Kumar, S. (2018). "Theorising Chinese international relations and understanding the rise of China: A preliminary investigation". *Relaciones Internacionales, 54*, 23–32.

Li, X. (2017). *Community with a shared future for mankind: A new solution for global governance*. Beijing: China Study Press.

Ling, L. H. M. (2016). "What's in name? A critical interrogation of the 'Chinese School of IR'". In Y. Zhang, & T. C. Chang (Eds.), *Constructing a Chinese school of international relations (Ongoing debates and sociological realities)*. London and New York: Routledge.

Liu, H. (2020). "Lun Xi Jinping fazhi sixiang zhong de guoji fa yaoyi" ("On the essentials of international law in Xi Jinping's thought of rule of law"). *Bijiao Fa Yanjiu (Comparative Law Studies), 6*, 1–13.

Mokry, S. (2018). "Decoding Chinese concepts for the global order. How Chinese scholars rethink and shape foreign policy ideas". In *Merics China monitor*. https://merics.org/en/report/decoding-chinese-concepts-global-order.

Morin, E. (2001). *I sette saperi necessari all'educazione del futuro*. Milano: Raffaello Cortina Editore.

Qin, Y. (2004). "The third culture: The integration of scientific and humanistic methods in IR research". In *World economics and politics* (Vol. 1). Beijing: Social Sciences Press.

Qin, Y. (2011a). Development of international relations theory in China: Progress through debates. *International Relations Affairs of the Asia-Pacific, 11*, 231–257.

Qin, Y. (2011b). Rule, rules, and relations: Towards a synthetic approach to governance. *Chinese Journal of International Politics, 4*(1), 117–145.

Ren, X. (2016). "The "Chinese School" debate: Personal reflections". In Y. Zhang, & T. C. Chang (Eds.), *Constructing a Chinese school of international relations (Ongoing debates and sociological realities)*. London and New York: Routledge.

Simonoff, A., & Briceño Ruiz, J. (2017). "La Escuela de la Autonomía, América Latina y la teoría de las relaciones internacionales". *Estudios Internacionales, 49*(186), 39–89.

Staiano, M. F., & Vadell, J. (2020). "China en los intersticios de la crisis del multilateralismo y la globalización neoliberal: La Franja y la Ruta en Europa y el caso italiano". *Araucaria. Revista Iberoamericana de Filosofía, Política, Humanidades y Relaciones Internacionales, 22*(45), 433–455.

Staiano, M. F., & Marcelli, F. (2020). "COVID-19全球疫情的挑战、反思与展望——以意大利为视角的观察" (Challenges, Reflections and prospects of the COVID-19 Global Pandemic. An observation from Italy's perspective). *Chinese Review of International Law (国际法研究编辑部国际法研究), 4*, 3–24.

Su, C. (2016). From Guanxi through Gongsheng: A cultural and institutional interpretation to China's diplomatic theory. *World Economics and Politics, 1*, 5–25.

Su, C. (2019). Zhongguo daguo waijiao de zhengzhi xue lilun jichu (The political theoretical basis of China's great power diplomacy). *Guoji Guangxi Lilun (International Relations Theory), 8*, 4–19.

Tan, C. (2015). "'Wangrencracy': China's great civilization-state model". In *China studies quarterly*. Shanghai.

Tang, S. (2013). *The social evolution of international politics.* Oxford University Press.

Tickner A. B. & Blaney D. L. (2013). *Claiming the international.* London and New York: Routledge.

Wang H. (2013). *The Rise of China and the Chinese International Relations Scholarship.* UK: Lexington Books.

Wang, S., & Hu, S. (2016). Gongsheng zhexue lun (Symbiosis philosophy outline). *Journal of Chang'an University (Social Science Edition), 18*(3), 71–84.

Yan, X. (2011). *Ancient Chinese thought, modern Chinese power*. New Jersey: Princeton University Press.

Yu, Z. (2005). "Yuxiang" (Introduction). In G. Shuyong (Ed.), *Guoji Guanxi: Huhuan Zhongguo lilun (International relations: Inviting a Chinese theory)* (pp. 121–132). Tianjin: Tianjin People's Publishing House.

Zhang Y. & Chang T. (2016). *Constructing a Chinese School of International Relations (Ongoing debates and sociological realities).* London and New York: Routledge.

Chapter 6
Symbols and Signs

The law has always represented the need for a culture of justice, that balance of interests often represented by a goddess holding a scale in her hand, capable of rebalancing opposing legal positions by generating a convergent and reconciling synthesis. The law is also the protection of juridical situations without protection and which society requests, progressively with the affirmation of its own self-determining needs. The law limits and enhances freedoms, disciplining them in juridical cases through which they can find action. The law, therefore, is a social science in the name of which general, abstract and obligatory rules are determined so that a peaceful and harmonious coexistence between individuals can be achieved. The construction of the rule of law derives precisely from this symbol of justice, equity, solidarity, the golden mean, humanity. One of the most evident signs of the rule of law are human rights, as fundamental, inalienable, non-transferable, non-suspendable rights, which precisely protect and preserve human dignity as an essential trait of the human being. The development of international human rights law under the aegis of the principle of equality is a recent achievement. From an anthropological perspective, however, human rights have presented themselves as a "Western dogma" (Supiot, 2012: 244): proof of this is not only the Christian philosophical dogma, but also the first declarations, for example the Universal Declaration of Human Rights of 12 December 1948, whose drafting was not attended by representatives of non-Western legal cultures. However, "in order for human rights to continue to perform a dogmatic function, its interpretation must evolve together with the historical development and with the geographical extension of the sciences and techniques, which supposes that non-Western people appropriate it and thus endangering their meaning and scope. Only in this way will human rights stop being a creed imposed on humanity and will return to being a common dogmatic resource open to everyone's interpretation" (Supiot, 2012: 245). Generating a community with a shared future for mankind has a strong juridical connotation, since the community, as a common duty *cum munus*, "has its origin in the law" and constitutes "a humanistic overlap between intersubjectivity and community" (Esposito, 2006).

M. F. Staiano, *Chinese Law and Its International Projection*, Understanding China,
https://doi.org/10.1007/978-981-19-9578-1_6

The Chinese legal experience, therefore, especially in the field of the creation of a rule of law, with its main corollary of the guarantee of fundamental human rights, appears to us as a necessity to deconstruct axiomatic terms of the contemporary legal structure. Chinese opera takes on a double direction: on the one hand, international law influencing Chinese domestic law; on the other hand, Chinese law—as a cumulative construction of foreign law, its own ethical traditions and rituals and internationalist principles—which returns to an international projection after being revitalised with new interpretations and innovative contents. The "lateral" and destructuring action of the Chinese interpretation represents a "strategy of peace" (Jullien, 2011: 34) necessary for a qualitative evolution of fundamental rights.

The Chinese commitment to the construction of integrative systems of the international order therefore proves to be necessary to get out of a reality crystallised in the *Homo homini lupus* which has characterised an involutionary stasis of international law and international relations. Development, cooperation, solidarity, the eradication of poverty, the realisation of the human person are common objectives of the international community which, despite constituting the foundations of the United Nations system, today seem to be contested in an increasingly polarised way.

Borrowing the definition of Gabriel Merino (2021), the current era is characterised by being in a state of "Hybrid and Fragmented World War": this hybridization of the war context is manifested with a multidimensionality of the implemented forms, involving communication, energy, the economy, in addition to the traditional methods of hard warfare. This structural feature of the global context became evident in full force with the situation in Ukraine, where there has been extreme polarisation between Russia and Ukraine. This clear division between good and evil, between the just defence and the criminal invasion, has subsequently incorporated other alliances, polarising them, without creating the conditions for a pacification of events. In fact, the revitalization of NATO and the creation of a pro-Ukraine and anti-Russia "Western united front" has crystallised into a mainstream that has not admitted alternative visions, with instrumentalization at the international level: we can frame the conflict Russia- Ukraine as a return to the ideological war between the West and the East. However, even polarisation, in reality, can always constitute an opportunity, if within the tension it is possible to grasp that prolific creativity typical of Chinese thought: in fact, in the Chinese language precisely "the tension between opposites defines many meanings" (Jullien, 2011).

For a long time, a change in the mainstream of international relations has been expected to be necessary, essentially based on an asymmetry between the hard power of a few central countries at the expense of many peripheral countries (Simonoff & Briceño Ruiz, 2017). In fact, "the social dimension of globalisation is condemned to remain a slogan if there are no appropriate institutional devices which allow the countries of the South to oppose their own interpretation of fundamental rights to that of the countries of the North" (Supiot: 279).

There are many calls for a "new type" "democratisation" of international relations for a fairer and more equitable international order. The most profound and articulated is undoubtedly the idea of generating a "community with a shared future for mankind", formulated by China and involving all aspects of international relations, understood as globality, in a multidimensional way. This purpose has also been marked in the XX Congress of the Communist Party of China, as well as exposed in the Report of President Xi Jinping, in particular in Chap. 14, where the connection between the structuring of the community with a shared future and the promotion of world peace and development (Xi, 2022).

Starting from the concept of Tianxia, in fact, we understand the global vocation of the Chinese proposal: "everything under heaven" indicates not only all the States, but also all the peoples and all the natural elements of the Earth. An animist vocation, we can say, that has been amalgamated through the cultural sedimentation of Taoism, Confucianism and Buddhism (Cheng, 2000). A convergence capable of generating the idea of a world-system and non-interstatuality (Zhao, 2022). This is the premise for understanding the community with a shared future: global, multidimensional issues that depend on common responsibility and prosperity. Therefore, not the sum of individual particular interests, not even a banal balance of interests, not a system of alliances with friends and enemies, but a community. This concept, moreover, materialised in the contemporary era when the United Nations was established, intended precisely as the institutionalisation of the "international community."

The idea of a constant exchange reveals an evolution imposed by Chinese theory and practice: not only an osmotic relationship between international law and domestic law, but also as a direct application in international relations. The idea of an integral law, with a comprehensive approach to the rule of law, is the representation of the need for a new *ius commune* that reorders a chaotic situation of "world disorder" from below as a global democratic instance.

Furthermore, the construction of a community with a shared future implies the existence of a community, in which all members must be welcomed and accepted, all visions must be discussed and taken into consideration to favour a fair exchange, a peaceful coexistence. Indeed, in political philosophy there is talk of a "correspondence between the semantics of the community with the crisis of subjectivity", since "the community discourse has an intersubjective foundation" (Esposito, 2006).

The community has the difficult task of "keeping ethics and politics in balance" and constitutes a goal that makes its symbolic strength of its impossibility (Esposito). After the severe financial crises, the transition from G7 to G20 meetings since 1999 seemed to have defined a world in which emerging economies were integrating the "industrialised economies", proposing new formats, new paths. The experience of the BRICS(A) countries also represents the need to give voice to new global demands. As stated by Supiot, "in the face of the globalisation of the market economy, mechanisms are needed that allow a human and social hermeneutic of economic law" (Supiot, 2012: 280).

In this sense, the Chinese initiatives BRI and GDI should be considered as hermeneutical practices. They represent not only a graphical, semiotic change, but of the meaning offered to the international community in terms of semantics of international relations. The global cooperation that these initiatives envisage, in fact, constitute innovative signals of permanent and unheeded needs by a "centrifugal north" which inexorably has to learn to coexist with a "centripetal south". The change of paradigms crystallised in the relationships of "hard-power" and "soft-power" is not easy but necessary. The communicative, military and political violence that characterises international relations in recent years is the manifesto of the resistance of traditionally powerful states to the demands for democratisation of international institutions. If we think that the anthropological birth of law is strenuously linked to violence (Supiot; Esposito: 23), we can therefore understand how the effort to build a community with a shared future, characterised by an increasingly cogent and internationalised integral law, represents a ideal solution in the current context of strong changes. The space of legal community therefore fills the interstices of violence that resist a reshaping of international balances.

We are faced with an undiscovered relationality, marked by new symbols, new revealing signs of other possible humanity, of other forgotten needs, of a radical deconstruction and reworking of the essential terms of the ethical and aesthetic community. In this sense, the alignment of the southern countries is driving an innovative opening, while the western countries are increasingly closed in their own self-proclaimed categories, symbolically visible from the physical walls and diplomatic barriers imposed in recent years.

In this context, international relations between China and Latin America, for example, are progressing. These are, in fact, at the centre of a highly controversial debate between the old Western geopolitics and the new theoretical schools of the global South.

We must overcome the temptation to observe international phenomena in the light of pre-established schemes, already mentioned, built in other times, with other knowledge based on certain cultural elements, now obsolete. The old structures reproduce, reappear, generating an "order" that appears immutable, absolute, and despite its imperfection and injustice, it has generated a consolidated ideology, especially in matters of international relations. We often speak of new "hegemonies" as the intention of a country to impose its ideological structures on other cultures, especially with reference to China.

International relations between China and Latin America and the Caribbean (LAC) are experiencing a very relevant historical moment. In 2008, China published its first Document on China's Policy towards Latin America and the Caribbean,[1] which sets out the pillars of relations between China and LAC[2] and already mentions what is the current "comprehensive strategic association" between China and some countries in the region: Brazil (2012), Peru (2013), Argentina (2014) and Venezuela (2014). It is a link that is based on a cooperative friendship between the countries that acts in an integral way, that is to say, that it goes through the political, the cultural, the economic-financial, the technological and the military. In November 2016, the merely

---

[1] PRC Government, *China's Policy Paper on Latin America and the Caribbean*, 2008, disponible en http://www.gov.cn/english/official/2008-11/05/content_1140347.htm.

[2] To deepen the themes of the 2008 Document in relation to the traditional principles of Guanxi see: Staiano M. F. & Others, *Estudios sobre la República Popular China: Relaciones internacionales y Política interna,* La Plata, Ediciones IRI-UNLP, 2016, pp. 65–69.

programmatic document of 2008 was superseded by a new Document,[3] which takes into account the experience of eight years of intense relations, anticipating a new stage of development of ties between China and LAC.

Already in the Prologue, emphasis is placed on globalisation[4] and multipolarity to achieve the difficult goals of "world peace and common development". Reference is also made to the need to "build international relations of a new type", with the win-win principle as the core and "to forge a community with a shared future for humanity". In this process, the purpose is to "bring the China-LAC international cooperation association to a New Height". "All countries, big or small, strong or weak, rich or poor, are all equal members of the international community." The most ambitious purpose is represented by the "closer heart and friendship between the peoples of China and LAC in order to make contributions to the harmonious coexistence of the various civilizations of the world", through "exchanges between peoples". According to Liu Huawen:

> The development of international democratisation, through the decolonization movement of the 1950s to 1970s and then through the economic development of countries in the past decades, have changed significantly. In terms of the international power configuration, the asymmetry of the absolute dominance of the Western developed countries no longer exists, and it is more realistic and feasible for developing countries to participate in multilateral international mechanisms on an equal footing politically, economically and legally as sovereign states and members of the United Nations. Even small and medium-sized countries can use international rules to assert their rights, make contributions to the global governance in areas such as climate change and sustainable development, and win support and victory under the framework of international law. This is unprecedented or uncommon in human history.
>
> (Liu, 2020).

If we think of the demands of the global South as proposals for a progressive and integrative transformation of the international order, through new relationships and interactions, we understand the importance of the Chinese example. Confucius said that one must have "the ability to govern and exercise power through culture". Culture as "cultivation of the self" 修身 (*Xiushen*) capable of practically "influencing" that of others through one's own behaviour. An osmotic, symbiotic culture, inspired by an anthropological juridical essence. The legal culture that has taken root in contemporary China, in line with that *homo juridicus* that has characterised man on a global level since ancient times (Supiot), is an innovative relaunch of the principle of legal effectiveness. Integral law represents the fusion of Western and Asian, African and Latin American legal culture: a widespread legal consciousness that regulates internal law, emanates internationally and raises awareness of international relations. It is always complex to be able to get out of a domination structure, especially if it is based on theories that have legitimised its concrete practices: "the invasive Western

---

[3] PRC Government, *China's Policy Paper on Latin America and the Caribbean*, 2016, disponible en http://www.fmprc.gov.cn/mfa_eng/zxxx_662805/t1418254.shtml.

[4] The issue of globalization has recently also been highlighted in a positive key, although in its economic dimension, by President Xi Jinping in his speech at the World Economic Forum Summit held in Davos in January 2017. Available at: https://www.weforum.org/agenda/2017/01/full-text-of-xi-jinping-keynote-at-the-world-economic-forum.

conceptual *koiné* increases the risk of "covering up" the Chinese tradition and making it unrecognisable, losing the possibility of capturing its most original and creative traits in it" (Sini, 2012: 57).

It is in this sense that the Chinese experience innovates from within the same structures, not disavowing them but recognizing their importance to reconstruct new meanings. The resulting enrichment of meaning is fundamental for building a "planetary" (Morin) community with a shared future.

References

Cheng, A. (2000). *Storia del pensiero cinese. Dalle origini allo "studio del mistero"*. Torino: Einaudi.

Esposito, R. (2006). *Communitas. Origine e destino della comunità.* Torino: Einaudi.

Jullien, F. (2011). *L'ansa e l'accesso. Strategie del senso in Cina, Grecia.* Milano-Udine: Mimesis Insegne.

Liu, H. (2020). "Lun Xi Jinping fazhi sixiang zhong de guoji fa yaoyi" ("On the essentials of international law in Xi Jinping's thought of rule of law"). *Bijiao fa yanjiu (Comparative Law Studies), 6*, 1–13.

Merino, G. E. (2021). Nuevo momento geopolítico mundial: La Pandemia y la aceleración de las tendencias de la transición histórico-espacial contemporánea. *Estudos Internacionais: Revista De relações Internacionais Da PUC Minas, 9*(4), 106–130. https://doi.org/10.5752/P.2317-773X.2021v9n4p106-130.

Morin, E. (2001). *I sette saperi necessari all'educazione del futuro.* Milano: Raffaello Cortina Editore.

Simonoff, A., & Briceño Ruiz, J. (2017). "La Escuela de la Autonomía, América Latina y la teoría de las relaciones internacionales". *Estudios Internacionales, 49*(186), 39–89.

Sini, C. (2012). *Il sapere dei segni. Filosofia e semiotica.* Milano: Editoriale Jaca Book S.r.l.

Supiot, A. (2012). *Homo juridicus. Ensayo sobre la función antropológica del derecho.* Siglo XXI Editores.

Xi, J. (2022). Report to the 20th national congress of the communist party of China October 16, 2022. In *Hold high the great banner of socialism with Chinese characteristics and strive in unity to build a modern socialist country in all respects.* https://www.fmprc.gov.cn/eng/zxxx_662805/202210/t20221025_10791908.html.

Zhao, T. (2022). "Tianxia 1.2", podcast by Gabriele Battaglia. Retrieved October 2, 2022, from https://www.rsi.ch/rete-due/programmi/cultura/laser/Tianxia-1.2-15662734.html?f=podcast-shows.

The manufacturer's authorised representative in the EU is Springer Nature Customer Service Centre GmbH, Europaplatz 3, 69115 Heidelberg, Germany. If you have any concerns regarding our products, please contact ProductSafety@springernature.com

Printed and bound by CPI Group (UK) Ltd, Croydon, CR0 4YY
30/09/2026
02225264-0004